*Twayne's English Authors Series*

*Thomas Hobbes*

TEAS 215

Courtesy of *The National Portrait Gallery, London*

# Thomas  Hobbes

# THOMAS HOBBES

By CHARLES H. HINNANT

*University of Missouri*

TWAYNE PUBLISHERS
A DIVISION OF G. K. HALL & CO., BOSTON

**Library of Congress Cataloging in Publication Data**

Hinnant, Charles H
    Thomas Hobbes.

    (Twayne's English authors series ; TEAS 215)
    Bibliography: p. 167–70
    Includes index.
    1. Hobbes, Thomas, 1588–1679.
B1247.H56          192          77–10616
ISBN  0–8057–6684–7

# Contents

About the Author

Preface

Acknowledgements

Chronology

1. Hobbes the Man      13

2. The Emerging Philosopher      32

3. *The Elements of Law*      44

4. *De Cive*      74

5. *Leviathan*      96

6. Hobbes and Critical Theory      132

7. The Legacy of Thomas Hobbes      146

Notes and References      159

Selected Bibliography      167

Index      171

# About the Author

Charles H. Hinnant received his B.A. at Princeton University, his M.A. and Ph.D. at Columbia University. His career as a teacher and scholar began in 1965 when he joined the faculty at the University of Michigan in Ann Arbor. He stayed at Michigan until 1972 when he came to the department of English at the University of Missouri in Columbia, where he has remained. In 1968 Professor Hinnant was the recipient of a National Endowment for the Humanities, Junior Fellowship, and in 1975 of a University of Missouri, Summer Research Grant. Although he has taught a wide range of courses in English and Comparative Literature, Professor Hinnant has also pursued specialized interests in seventeenth and eighteenth century literature and in interdisciplinary studies. He has published articles in *The Michigan Academician,* in *Studies in Philology, Renaissance Quarterly, English Language Notes, Criticism, Eighteenth-Century Studies,* and *Clio.* The subjects of these studies include John Milton, Andrew Marvell, John Dryden, William Hogarth, Thomas Gray, and Thomas Hobbes, and have touched on such diverse areas as the history of art, seventeenth century philosophy, Augustan historiography, and critical theory. Of his essay, entitled "Marvell's Gallery of Art," Pierre Legouis has written that "it stands apart from the common run of papers on this poet." Professor Hinnant is presently at work on a book on William Congreve.

# Preface

This book is intended to be an incentive to those who wish to explore Hobbes's thought. The details of his achievement remain to be discovered at closer quarters — in the texts themselves. To give this introduction as broad an appeal as possible, it seemed best to approach Hobbes's works for their own sake and not to try to relate them to specific academic disciplines. This task is made easier by Hobbes's own practice. Although his terminology is sufficiently clear and precise to appeal to the specialist, his major works were addressed for the most part to an educated general public. In this I have tried to follow him.

Hobbes's thought displays perhaps a greater degree of internal consistency than that of any other political theorist of comparable eminence. *De Cive* (1642) and *Leviathan* (1650) unfold, without significant alteration, from the pattern established in Hobbes's first important political treatise, *The Elements of Law* (1640). Consequently, students of Hobbes's political theory have relied primarily upon a thematic approach: the explanation of his political ideas has been sought either in *Leviathan* or in the unity of his thought as it might be reconstructed from all three books. I have tried to proceed by a somewhat different route. The book begins with a short account of Hobbes's life and career and proceeds in chapter two to set forth a theory concerning the implications of his conversion to philosophy. This discussion provides the background for the next three chapters wherein I try to trace the evolution of Hobbes's thought from *The Elements of Law* through *De Cive* to *Leviathan*. Only one chapter is entirely devoted to a consideration of Hobbes's masterpiece. The last two chapters deal successively with Hobbes's contribution to critical theory and with the contours of his influence on English literature.

Thus the emphasis of this book has been placed upon the relations of each treatise to its author and his audience. My intention has been to establish clearly that Hobbes's aims in his political writings move through three distinct phases. In the first phase (*The Ele-*

*ments of Law*), Hobbes seeks to erect a system that will be above dispute. He soon comes, however, to recognize the impossibility of this goal and seeks (in *De Cive*) simply to minimize as much as possible the controversial aspects of his theory. At the same time we become increasingly conscious in reading the English translation of *De Cive* of an author behind the argument manipulating our responses. In the third phase (*Leviathan*), Hobbes emerges into full view as an ironist and publicist for his own ideas, abandoning any hope of mitigating the polemical aspects of his thought. Without assuming that the changing relations between Hobbes's aims and his prose in these works lead to inconsistencies in his arguments, this study will try to show that the distinctive character of each work is to a large extent determined by the way it fits into the pattern of his growth as a philosopher.

In these chapters I deal with Hobbes not as a cosmic system builder but as a philosopher of man and society. How far can the two elements be separated? My own assumption is that Hobbes's political theory can be considered without extensive reference to his philosophy of nature. The reason is that only the epistemological and methodological parts of Hobbes's system can be shown to have any bearing on his political thought. It might be argued that the main elements of Hobbes's natural philosophy were already worked out in *A Short Tract on First Principles* (circa 1630), long before he had devoted much attention to politics and to religion, and were subsequently projected onto the broader political concerns. But that argument would be cogent only if the metaphysical hypothesis inspired by his early studies of bodies in motion had more than a general influence on his political theory. Without denying the importance of *De Corpore,* on which Hobbes apparently labored for a number of years as the first part of his system (which he hoped would confirm his reputation as a New Philosopher), the basic structure of Hobbes's political theory can perhaps best be studied in terms of his early conception of his role as a Humanist scholar in the service of those who governed society.

Perhaps nothing serves to bring out the humanistic aspects of Hobbes's political thought more emphatically than the controversy it aroused. To the religious of his age, many of his arguments — especially his assertion that in a well-ordered society the civil sovereign must be regarded as the source of all values — were seen as the workings of the devil. For his insistence upon the fragility of all human institutions he was later condemned by those who believed in a natural harmony between private interest and public good. In the twentieth-century, he has been credited with discovering in the Biblical image of Leviathan a profound symbol for the overwhelming power of the modern national state. There has hardly been any period from the seventeenth century onward which has not found some aspect of Hobbes's political thought provocative or repellant. But the arguments which he set forth could hardly have provoked such a response were they not elements of a vision of politics that has some relevance to man's condition. Hobbes asserted emphatically what earlier political thinkers had only intimated: that political societies are collective bodies which have their own laws of existence. As a humanist, Hobbes held that man must obey these laws, for their purpose is to prevent the body politic from dissolving into what Hobbes, in a famous phrase, described as a war of every man against every man. The consequences of this view — a recognition of the need for political cohesion and the conviction that a lasting society must be based upon a "real unity"of men — have insured Hobbes a permanent place in the history of political philosophy. In the history of science, he may have played only a small part; in political theory, he changed the course of modern thought and opened up new directions for others.

CHARLES H. HINNANT

*University of Missouri*

# Acknowledgements

During the years I have been at work on this book, I have been extremely fortunate in the assistance I have received from a number of people and to them I should like to express my gratitude. To begin with, I am especially indebted to Professor T.S.K. Scott-Craig of Dartmouth College, whose thoughtful advice provided much of the initial impetus and inspiration for this book. I also wish to thank Professors Sheridan Baker, William Holtz and John Middendorf for their generous encouragement and support. I would also like to acknowledge the research facilities and assistance offered to me by the staffs of the Baker Library, Dartmouth College, and of Ellis Library at the University of Missouri. I also wish to express my gratitude to Mrs. Corinne Davis who typed the manuscript. Lastly, I would like to thank the editors of *Criticism* and the Wayne State University Press for graciously allowing me to use, as part of the sixth chapter of this book, an essay that first appeared in the winter issue, 1976, of their journal.

# Chronology

1588  April 5, Thomas Hobbes born in Westport adjoining Malmesbury in North Wiltshire, England.

1596  Hobbes attends Malmesbury School.

1603  Enters Magdalen Hall, Oxford.

1608  Takes his bachelor degree and becomes tutor to William Cavendish, eldest son of Sir William Cavendish, later the first Earl of Devonshire.

1610  Hobbes and Cavendish make the grand tour, visiting France and Italy.

1628  The translation of Thucydides' *The History of the Peloponnesian Wars* is published.

1628  June 20, Hobbes's friend and patron dies; the straitened circumstances of the widowed countess require her to dispense with Hobbes's services.

1629  Hobbes's second visit to the continent as travelling tutor to the son of Sir Gervase Clinton. In the course of the journey he discovers Euclid's *Elements*.

1631  Hobbes recalled from Paris to become tutor to William Cavendish, third Earl of Devonshire, the eldest son of his old master; Devonshire remains Hobbes's patron for the remainder of his life.

1634  Accompanying the young Earl, Hobbes makes his third visit to the continent. He meets Galileo in Florence and is received into the scientific circle of Mersenne in Paris. Sometime during this period the undated *Short Tract* is composed.

1637  Hobbes returns to England.

1640  *The Elements of Law* is circulated privately in manuscript. Fearing reprisal from Parliament, Hobbes flees from London to Paris.

1641  Hobbes renews friendship with Mersenne. The "Objections" to Descartes' *Meditations* are published.

1642   *De Cive* published abroad in Latin. Begins work on *Leviathan*.

1644   "Tractatus Opticus" published in Paris by Mersenne in *Cogitata Physico-Mathematica*.

1646   Hobbes becomes mathematical instructor to the Prince of Wales, later Charles II.

1647   Hobbes seriously ill with a fever.

1650   *The Answer to Davenant's Preface before Gondibert. The Elements of Law* is published in two separate parts, the epistemological section under the title *Human Nature* in February; the political section under the title *De Corpore Politico* in May.

1651   Hobbes returns from Paris to London, making peace with the Council of State. *Leviathan* published, *De Cive* reissued in English under the title *Philosophical Rudiments concerning Government and Society*.

1654   *Of Liberty and Necessity,* Hobbes's reply to a discourse by Bishop Bramhall, published without his consent.

1655   *De Corpore,* the intended first part of Hobbes's comprehensive system, is published.

1656   *The Questions concerning Liberty, Necessity and Chance.*

1658   *De Homine,* the second part of Hobbes's philosophical scheme is published.

1660   Restoration of Charles II. At the King's command, Hobbes granted royal favor and a pension.

1668   Hobbes writes *Behemoth: the History of the Causes of the Civil Wars of England.* Publication forbidden by the King.

1669   Hobbes visited by the Grand Duke of Tuscany. *Dialogue between a Philosopher and a Student of the Common Laws of England.*

1673   "The Travels of Ulysses."

1675   The full translation of *The Odyssey.*

1676   *The Iliad.*

1679   *Behemoth* is published with Hobbes's consent. Hobbes dies. Buried at the Parish Church of Hault Hucknall, near Hardwick Hall in Derbyshire.

1683   *De Cive, Leviathan* and other "Pernicious Books and Damnable Doctrines" proscribed by the University of Oxford and ordered to be publicly burnt.

CHAPTER 1

# *Hobbes the Man*

OF the major philosophers, Hobbes is perhaps the most entangled in myth. A long tradition, already underway in his own lifetime and continued for many years afterwards, made Hobbes into a legendary — and thus larger than life — antagonist in the heroic struggle of Christianity against atheism. Much of the magnification of his personality was the result of the impassioned response of his contemporaries to the skeptical and relativist implications of his philosophy. The very imagery of Hobbes's greatest work, *Leviathan,* was adopted by critics who sought to vilify his character. It must be added, however, that Hobbes himself contributed to this attitude. In a century of schools and movements, Hobbes was a confirmed individualist who resolutely pursued the implications of his own ideas to their logical conclusion, regardless of the consequences. His courage, his obstinacy, his charm and wit, and even his longevity made it inevitable that he would become the object of veneration or damnation. Any serious revaluation of the philosopher, therefore, has always sought to extricate his writings, his friendships, and his character from the legends which surrounded him. In contrast to the traditional "bête noire" of his age, modern commentators have seen Hobbes as a philosopher with the rare gifts of insight and imagination combined with the ability to write with elegance and pungency.

## I  *Hobbes's Early Life*

There is little in the relatively modest circumstances of his birth, family and youth to indicate a mythical Hobbes, the apostle of infidelity and "bug-bear to the nation." However, Hobbes's own inclination to myth-making led him, in a verse *Autobiography* com-

13

posed in the last year of his life, to add to his own legend. Hobbes was supposed by his contemporaries to suffer excessively from fears and perturbations. In his autobiography he ascribes this trait half-whimsically, half-seriously to the circumstances surrounding his birth, which occurred during the year of the Spanish Armada. Hobbes was born on Good Friday, April 5, 1588, in the village of Westport near Malmesbury in Wiltshire. The village was rife with rumors of an impending invasion when Hobbes was born, and he wrote that his mother "was big with such fear that she brought twins to birth, myself and fear at the same time."[1] It was fear, Hobbes added, that taught him to detest the enemies of his country and to "ever serve Peace" (11. 27–28).

Hobbes also commemorated the history and antiquities of the town from which he had emancipated himself. In this exercise in civic piety, he recalled that Malmesbury had "many things worth mentioning" (1.9). There was the tomb of heroic Athelstane who led the English in defending their land against the Danes. There was the Latin school, the first in England, which was established by Adhelm. As a young man Hobbes may have responded to the imaginative appeal of these glories of a vanished age. It is not impossible that Athelstane's patriotism and Adhelm's love of Latin influenced his writings.

Hobbes has little to say of his own ancestors but his admiring biographer, John Aubrey, reports that his father was a vicar of Westport and Charlton.[2] A choleric man, Thomas Hobbes the Elder was, in Aubrey's words, "one of the Clergie of Queen Elizabeth's time — a little Learning went a great way with him and many other ignorant Sir Johns in those days; could only read the prayers of the Church and the homilies; and disesteemed Learning . . . as not knowing the Sweetnes of it" (147). After an altercation with the parson who succeeded him at Westport, Hobbes's father was forced to flee, abandoning home and family; subsequently he died in obscurity "beyound [sic] London, about 80 yeares since" (148).

Such an upheaval in his childhood could not fail to have a decisive influence on his later life and work. If a sense of insecurity about human existence in general is part of Hobbes's outlook, it may have been implanted in the uncertainty of the home where he acquired his first impressions of the world. Aware as he was of the unpredictability of events, Hobbes's response to the immediate moment was seldom spontaneous. Even as a child he may have been pessimistic. Though he "was playsome enough," according to Aubrey, there was "even then a contemplative Melancholinesse" in his mien (148–149). It was not to be expected that a melancholic boy of "yellowish" complexion should participate in the boisterous conviviality of school life; as a student Hobbes "would gett him into a corner, and learn his Lesson by heart presently" (149).

However, Hobbes was not so insecure as to be incapable of pleasure. He was always loved "for his pleasant facetiousness and good-nature" (153), and his fortunes early took a turn for the better. Sometime before he was four years old, his father's brother, Francis Hobbes, who was a wealthy glover and alderman, assumed responsibility for the upbringing of Thomas Hobbes the Elder's children. He arranged to have Hobbes's brother Edmund — who "resembled him in aspect" but was simply "a good plain under-standing countrey-man" in intellect — apprenticed in the glove trade (148). He assisted Thomas, the younger son, to enter school, paying all of the fees for his education. Both sons were remembered in their uncle's will. Frances Hobbes thus deserves credit as the first of a series of paternal figures whose protection and support helped to make Hobbes's subsequent career possible.

At the age of four Hobbes began his schooling at Westport Church but was soon forced to leave when the church was painted. He continued his studies at Malmesbury, then at a private school in Westport where he was taught by Robert Latimer, a young man of nineteen and "a good Graecian" — "the first," writes Aubrey, "that came into our Parts hereabout since the Reformation" (148). Under Latimer's tutelage, Hobbes became proficient in both Latin and Greek. Although he made some uncomplimentary statements about his later scholastic education at college, Hobbes never lost his love for classical languages and literature. A lost translation of Euripides' *Medea* from Greek into Latin is indicative of his interest in both languages. This early endeavor may not have revealed any literary ability, but it is an indication of the humane scholarship for which Hobbes has always been respected.

At fourteen he was sent by his uncle to Magdalen College, Oxford. His studies were the usual ones for the university of his day, based primarily on scholastic logic and physics. Like many of his contemporaries, Hobbes displayed a distrust of scholastic learning, though he regarded himself as a "good Disputant" (149). Not surprisingly he preferred to devote his time to rereading the classics, which had been his earlier interest. Like other young men at the beginning of the seventeenth century, he became interested in old maps. Hobbes's explanation of his passion for this subject reveals something of the enthusiasm that was to sustain him in all his later pursuits: "... I fed my mind ... on maps celestial and maps terrestrial, and as I gazed on the painted constellations I rejoiced to companion the sun on his travels and to observe the art with which he apportions the days justly to all mankind. I observed, too, where Drake and Cavendish had cast a girdle round Neptune's waist and the different regions they had visited" (11.55–60).

## II  *The Humanist Scholar*

At the appropriate age of twenty, after completing a Bachelor of Arts degree, Hobbes was recommended by Sir James Hussee, his master at Magdalen Hall, to William Cavendish, Baron Hardwick and subsequently first Earl of Devonshire, as tutor to his son. Hobbes's connection with the Cavendish family as well as his warm friendship with their son, whom he served for twenty years, lasted throughout his life. Friendship and service were intimately bound up in Hobbes's relations with the Cavendish family. He was originally chosen for his youth, instead of a "grave Doctor" and "was his Lordship's page, and rose a hunting and hawking with him and kept his privy-purse" (149). Hobbes was even "sent ... up and downe to borrow money" for his lordship who was too ashamed to speak for himself (153). On the other hand, Hobbes's friendship with young Cavendish did not represent a retreat from earlier humanistic interests but rather the natural fulfillment of them. Although Aubrey speculates that "by this way of life he had almost forgott his Latin" (149), Hobbes's enthusiastic praise of the family library and of the books supplied to him to continue his studies proves that the patronage of the Cavendish family gave him the leisure and material security to pursue his inclination. His association with the Cavendish family also provided him the opportunity to travel abroad. Visiting the continent in 1610, on the first of four trips to Europe, Hobbes acquired a passable acquaintance with French and German and a first encounter with the wider political world. Leisure and security proved beneficial, for it was from this period that the publication of Hobbes's first work, his translation of Thucydides' *History of the Peloponnesian Wars* can be dated.

Hobbes's translation of Thucydides' *History* grew directly out of his relations with the Cavendish family. In continuation of Renaissance humanistic tradition, Hobbes conceived of his role as tutor and scholar as entailing responsibility to those who governed society. Throughout his life, whether as translator or as philosopher, Hobbes never abandoned this traditional social responsibility of the humanist scholar. In the sixteenth and early seventeenth centuries, English scholars had produced an immense body of translations from modern and classical languages. The idea that such translations could serve an educative purpose had thus been established well before Hobbes's time. This idea lies behind Sir Thomas North's *Plutarch* (1579), George Chapman's *Homer* (1616) and leads to the prodigious output of Philemon Holland (1552-1637) whose translations, as Thomas Fuller said, made a library of historians for the country gentry[3] — Livy (1600), Pliny's *Natural History* (1601), Plutarch's *Moralia* (1603), Suetonius (1606), Ammianus Marcellinus (1609), Camden's *Brittania* (1610) and Xenophon's *Cyropaedia* (1632). In translating Thucydides' *History of the Peloponnesian Wars,* Hobbes confirmed his own standing as a humanist scholar who drew enrichment from classical history at the same time that he carried on the humanist crusade for the classical tradition, its aristocratic polity and ethical values, and its ideals of heroic courage and magnanimity. For him as for North, Chapman, and Holland, the classical authors were a source of political wisdom: Thucydides, he wrote, "taught me how stupid democracy is and by how much one man is wiser than an assembly" (1.106). More explicitly than anywhere else Hobbes revealed in this translation his basic preferences, his humanistic orientation as well as his permanent obsession with the riddle of political institutions.

Having established himself in the Cavendish family as a tutor and scholar, Hobbes was not long in acquiring friends, among them two of England's greatest authors Francis Bacon and Ben Jonson. Edward Herbert, later Baron of Cherbury, was also an early friend who was doubtless acquainted with Hobbes through his master. He wrote a philosophical treatise, *De Veritate* (1624) which anticipated Hobbes's later rationalistic critique of religion. As the leading poet of his age, Jonson was seen at the Cavendish house. Because of the habit, common in the century, of circulating literary works in manuscript form prior to publication, the story that the dedication to the translation of Thucydides' *History* was not published until it was submitted to Ben Jonson and the Scottish poet Sir Robert Aytoun (LW, I, xxv), has generally been accepted. More doubt centers on Hobbes's relations with Sir Francis Bacon whose commitment to observation and experiment places him in an entirely different scientific tradition than Hobbes and who — unlike William Harvey, Galileo Galilei, Johannes Kepler and René Descartes — is never mentioned in Hobbes's writings as one of the founders, before himself, of the new philosophy.[4] Yet Hobbes might well have been acquainted with Bacon who was a friend of his master and who, divested of his political offices, devoted himself during the years between 1621 and 1626 entirely to writing and scientific pursuits.

These, then, may have been Hobbes's earliest friends. All of them were of quite different philosophical and literary persuasions, but all had at least one thing in common — their dedication to humanistic learning and humane culture.

### III  *Hobbes and the New Philosophy*

The first Earl of Devonshire died in 1626, the second in 1628. Because of financial difficulties, the Earl's widow was forced to dispense with Hobbes's services for a time, and he therefore agreed to accompany the son of Sir Gervase Clinton on a tour of the continent. By November, 1630, however, Hobbes had returned to the service of the Cavendish family and devoted the next seven years, by his own account, to teaching the third Earl of Devonshire the rudiments of logic, rhetoric, Latin, and geography (11.96–98). Hobbes's service to the family included a third and prolonged visit to Europe with his pupil where they "saw many cities of Italy and France and visited the sweet valleys of Savoy" (1.10). Hobbes must have been acquainted with the discoveries of Galileo and the European scientific community earlier, but on this trip the new science took hold of his mind and implanted within it ideas of the nature of motion and of its relation to visible appearances. These concepts would grow in Hobbes's thought, tying in with his humanistic interests, until he made them completely, almost idiosyncratically, his own.

Hobbes has been seen as a grave philosopher who attempted to adapt the insights of the new science to the investigation of philosophical problems and no doubt he was, but his own account of his initial meditations on motion lays stress on the sense of mystery which it evoked in his mind: "But whether on ship, or coach, or horse-back, my mind constantly pondered the nature of things; and it seemed to me that in the whole world only one thing is real, falsified though it be in many ways. One thing only is real, but it forms the basis of the things we falsely claim to be something, though they are only like the fugitive shapes of dreams or like the images I can multiply at will by mirrors; fantasies, creatures of our brains and nothing more, the only inner reality of which is motion" (11.112–120). If these lines seem to conjure up the visionary intensity of the convert, it should be remembered that Aubrey describes Hobbes's sudden change from scholar to philosopher as the result of an intellectual experience — the vivid impression made on him by Euclid's *Elements:* "Being in a Gentleman's Library, Euclid's Elements lay open, and 'twas the 47 *El. libri* I. He read the Propositions. *By G--,* sayd he (he would now and then sweare an emphaticall Oath by way of emphasis) *this is impossible!* So he reads the Demonstration of it, which referred him back to such a Proposition; which proposition he read . . . *Et sic deinceps* (and so on) that at last he was demonstratively convinced of that trueth. This made him in love with Geometry" (150).

The implications of Aubrey's anecdote is that geometry supplied a framework for all of Hobbes's future studies, a framework which was never again altered. Hobbes emerged with a passionate belief in the rationalism of the new science. Geometry was the foundation of this belief. Yet in his eager acceptance of scientific method and in his eager quest for knowledge, in his dogmatism and note of certitude, Hobbes conveys an impression of something forced, something that often marks the enthusiasm of the convert. When reading Galileo, Descartes, Gottfried Wilhelm von Leibniz, and Isaac Newton, we know, whatever the limits of their philosophy may be, that we are in contact with the entire man. When reading Hobbes we may feel that a philosopher who is always honest and often brilliant has gained knowledge at the expense of fullness and that our satisfaction in his philosophical procedures remains incomplete.

Hobbes's conversion to philosophy may be partially explained by the extraordinary latitude his position as a tutor allowed him. Hobbes not only had ample leisure time on his travels, but while in

France he moved in the highest social and intellectual circles. He cultivated the French scientists through his philosophical mentor, Marin Mersenne. A monk of the Franciscan order of the Minimi, Mersenne was universally admired for his scientific enthusiasm as well as for his piety and religious orthodoxy. From 1619 onward, Mersenne had gathered about him a circle of distinguished and learned men who met regularly in his cell to discuss astronomy, physics, mathematics, ethics, and cosmology. Mersenne was eager to encourage anyone with a scientific inclination and scientific interests. Hobbes paid specific debt to this French influence in his verse autobiography when he referred to Mersenne's clear style and ability to illuminate any problem brought to him. Mersenne's influence may have been first reflected in the undated early *Short Tract on First Principles*.[5] In this work, which was left unfinished, Hobbes gave the first rudimentary formulation to his views on metaphysics, optics, and ethics.

The years in which Hobbes was travelling with his pupil in France and Italy were thus far from stagnant. According to Anthony Wood, he was a regular attendant at the meetings of Mersenne's circle. He knew Pierre Gassendi and became acquainted through Mersenne with the ideas of Descartes. By all accounts, Mersenne regarded Hobbes not only as a philosopher of ability but as an intimate friend. It may have been Mersenne in fact who inspired Hobbes to undertake the vast project of developing a unified system that would encompass three great divisions of philosophy; of body, of man, and of society. In the year 1636 Hobbes also visited Galileo's villa at Arcetri near Florence; through Galileo he cultivated Claudius Berigardus, professor of philosophy at Pisa. Galileo's ideas were a fundamental influence on Hobbes's later political outlook as they were prevalent in all the scientific circles in which Hobbes moved. Galileo's distrust of the Aristotelian and medieval science of mechanics, his preoccupation with motion, force, and resistance provided the frame of reference in which Hobbes could develop his analysis of man and society. When Hobbes returned to England in 1637, he was ready, as he put it, "to be numbered among the philosophers" (1.134).

After his return to England, Hobbes continued to live with the Cavendish family, even though the young Earl of Devonshire had completed his courses of study. Hobbes's social and intellectual life in England merged comfortably at Great Tew, the country home of

Devonshire's brilliant young friend, Lucius Carey, Lord Falkland. There could have been few more impressive gatherings in England than those housed at Great Tew: Hobbes, Falkland, William Chillingworth, George Sandys, John Selden, Edward Hyde (later Earl of Clarendon), John Earle, George Morley, and Gilbert Sheldon. A large number of the visitors at Great Tew were of the aristocracy and clergy. Their interests were thus those of King and Church. This bias may have been the abiding influence that Hobbes derived from his visits to Great Tew. It is no surprise to find that Hobbes's commitment to serve the understanding of the contemporary political situation was the source for his first important philosophical work. This was *The Elements of Law* which was composed in English about this time, and which anticipated the central concerns of *De Cive* and *Leviathan*. According to Hobbes, the intent of *The Elements of Law* was to justify absolutism "in the light of first principles" and in such a way that "the whole argument might have the permanence of a strong chain" (11.136–138).

Seen in this light, *The Elements of Law* acquires an added dimension. Under the impact of the new philosophy, Hobbes turned from humanist history to scientific theory, from historical *exempla* to universal axioms; but in *The Elements of Law* he drew from them not merely a theoretical discussion of the various forms of government but practical advice for the conduct of politics. It would be well for those who tend to see Hobbes only as a doctrinaire materialist and determinist to remember that his "little treatise in English" was composed, as Aubrey puts it, "to demonstrate, that the sayd Powers and Rights were inseparably annexed to the Soveraignty, which soveraignty they did not then deny to be in the King" (151). Such a passage makes it clear that in thinking about politics Hobbes did not content himself with a demonstration of general principles but insisted that these principles serve as a guide to politics.

Hobbes's conversion was thus by no means total. If he temporarily abandoned humanistic learning and humanistic wisdom, he did not abandon humanistic inspiration, nor was he ever to do so completely. As the earlier period of his production was characterized by the publication of his translation of Thucydides's history, this period saw the publication of *The Elements of Law* and *De Cive*. Hobbes altered his mode but could not change his genius which was humanistic and political, not scientific and mathematical. Perhaps the clearest evidence of Hobbes's awareness of his humanistic aims was his belief that the circulation of *The Elements of Law* in manuscript endangered his position at home. Fearing reprisal, Hobbes fled in 1640 from England to France.

Hobbes's hasty flight has given rise to considerable scholarly speculation. Some consider it simply as evidence of Hobbes's long-standing royalist sentiment; others attribute it to the extraordinary timidity that led Hobbes to give an absolute preeminence to self-preservation in his political writings. Hobbes himself admitted that "he was the first of all that fled."[6] But whatever may have been its initial inspiration, Hobbes's return to Paris is not all that surprising. Galileo had been condemned by the Inquisition seven years earlier for maintaining in print that the earth moves around the sun. Descartes had suppressed his treatise on cosmology, *Le Monde,* in the following year and had voluntarily exiled himself to Holland. As a leading representative of the new philosophy in England, it was in a way fitting that Hobbes exiled himself to Paris, where he was assured of a warm welcome from Mersenne and his circle.

Hobbes's years in France were more than a romantic adventure, however. Apart from *The Elements of Law,* Hobbes's major philosophical works, as well as a number of minor pieces, were written in Paris where he lived almost continuously from 1640 to 1650. In Paris he began attending the meetings of Mersenne's group again, while keeping in touch with English affairs through correspondence and conversation with friends. The fruits of his first few years included a further expansion of his political theory. This work was printed privately in 1642 in Paris under the title *De Cive* as the last of three parts of his planned system. Hobbes also returned to his scientific research, composing the first draft of what was later called *De Corpore.* According to Hobbes, this work would have been ready for publication if it were not for the delay caused by a serious illness in 1647. During this period Hobbes composed several minor works. A criticism of Descartes' *Meditations* was included in *The Objections and Replies* published at Mersenne's behest with the *Meditations* in 1641. Hobbes also contributed the "Praefatio" and part of Proposition XXIV to Mersenne's *Ballistica* in 1644 and the seventh book of Mersenne's *Cogitata Physico-Mathematica* in the same year. He also completed a draft of an optical treatise by 1646.

Hobbes continued to engage in scientific research throughout this period, but the death of Falkland and another friend Sidney Godolphin in the English Civil War and the appearance of numerous Royalist exiles in Paris made it clear that Hobbes could not leave off his preoccupation with politics. Accordingly, he planned a new edition of *De Cive* with additional notes in answer to objections and a magisterial "Preface to the Reader." The edition was formally published in 1647 by a French physician and admirer Samuel Sorbière at the Elzevir Press in Amsterdam. A need for a systematic exposition of his political theory in English — with an expanded section of the relation of church and state — led Hobbes to compose his masterpiece *Leviathan,* which was completed in 1651.

In France, Hobbes also wrote *Of Liberty and Necessity.* Though composed in 1646 as the outcome of his debate on free will with John Bramhall, the refugee Bishop of Derry, this treatise was not published until 1652, when a pirated edition was printed without Hobbes's consent. Not all of Hobbes's time was spent debating and writing, however. As a measure of his reputation as a philosopher, Hobbes was invited to become mathematical instructor to the young Prince of Wales, later Charles II, who fled from England to Paris in 1646 after the defeat of the Royalist forces in the battle of Worcester. Hobbes's service to the Prince of Wales cannot have lasted beyond his illness in 1647 which continued for several months and almost brought an end to his life. Hobbes's attitude toward death during this crisis is an excellent example of the religious assumptions underlying the surface ambiguities of his thought. In his Latin prose autobiography, the emphasis is not upon suffering but upon the resolute piety of the philosopher who rejected Mersenne's generous offer of Roman Catholic absolution so that he might receive the proper sacrament of the Anglican Church (LW, I, xvi).

There was a marked decrease in Hobbes's philosophical activity after his unexpected recovery from his illness. Besides the infirmities of age — Hobbes was then sixty-one — the death of Mersenne in September 1648 and the subsequent dispersal of his group may explain Hobbes's temporary indifference to his writing. It was not long before Hobbes once again returned to England. In 1650 he arrived in London where he immediately made peace with the Council of State.

The timing of Hobbes's return, like that of his departure, has aroused controversy. The fact that it was followed by the publication of *Leviathan* led two of Hobbes's opponents to charge that *Leviathan* was "written in defence of Oliver's title" and "as a sly address to Cromwell."[7] There is some truth to this charge. A leatherbound copy of *Leviathan* was first presented to Charles II in Paris and the unwelcome reception it received from the King's associates prompted Marchamont Needham's *Mercurius Politicus* to report on 5 January 1651–1652 that "Mr. Hobbes declines in credit with his friends there of the Royal stamp."[8] More important, Hobbes's ideas coincided with those of a prominent group of *de facto* theorists who were not averse to the Commonwealth. To persuade Presbyterians and Royalists to support the new government, they used an argument that was similar to Hobbes's view that conquest gives a valid title to allegiance.[9] Hobbes himself boasted in 1656 that *Leviathan* "framed the minds of 1000 gentlemen to obedience to the new regime" (EW, VII, 336). On the other hand, Cromwell was not yet Lord Protector in 1651, and Hobbes insisted that it was fear of the French clergy that made him return to England. The latter argument is supported by Hobbes's attack upon Popery in the last section of *Leviathan*.

Whatever the reason for his return to England, Hobbes was at the height of his contemporary reputation in the years immediately following his arrival. In 1650 Hobbes's earliest philosophical work dealing with politics, *The Elements of Law,* was published in two distinct parts, the first entitled *Human Nature or the Fundamental Elements of Policy,* the second called *De Corpore Politico or the Elements of Law, Moral and Politic.* In the next year, shortly before publication of *Leviathan,* Hobbes issued an English translation of *De Cive* under the title of *Philosophical Rudiments concerning Government and Society.* It was in the same year that Hobbes found time to write and publish his famous *Answer to Davenant's Preface before Gondibert.* Hobbes's years of relative fame were not to last, however, for his later years were also those of greatest conflict. Even when *Leviathan* was published its views were revolutionary, and as time passed and its implications became clearer and were applied by Hobbes's adversaries to contemporary situations, Hobbes became embroiled in a series of increasingly violent controversies.

### IV    *The Later Years: Hobbes as Polemicist*

In England Hobbes lived in London for a while, but returned in 1653 to Derbyshire where he renewed acquaintance with his old patron, the third Earl of Devonshire. Here he hoped to turn his energies wholly to his scientific studies, but he was soon caught up in the two great disputes in which he allowed himself to become involved — the quarrel with the Oxford mathematicians and the altercation with the English clergy. Both controversies are much too involved in all their phases and ramifications to relate in detail here. An outspoken critic of Oxford University in *Leviathan,* Hobbes placed himself in a position which made it difficult for him to defend himself because he was not aware of the advances that had taken place there since his college days fifty years earlier. Indeed, his own insufficient training in the sciences at college was used by his Oxford adversaries to prove their point. In *Vindiciae Academiarium,* Seth Ward, professor of astronomy at Oxford and later Bishop of Exeter, accused Hobbes not only of having as little knowledge of the present state of English universities as one of the seven sleepers but of having stolen his optical theories from another man.

It was *De Corpore,* however, that drew the strongest fire from Hobbes's Oxford critics. While *De Corpore* — which Hobbes finally completed and published in 1655 — was devoted primarily to an exposition of Hobbes's metaphysical theories, the twentieth chapter tried to solve the ancient conundrum of the squaring of the circle. To his critics, this futile enterprise revealed not only defectiveness of method but great naïveté as well. Hobbes clearly failed to perceive his own limitations as a mathematician. In the *Exercitatio epistolica* of 1656, Ward ridiculed Hobbes's solution, but he had already been preceded by John Wallis, Savilian professor of geometry at Oxford and one of the leaders of English science during the second half of the seventeenth century. Within three months after the publication of *De Corpore,* Wallis launched a slashing attack on Hobbes's mathematical pretensions in a work entitled *Elenchus Geometriae Hobbiania.* Unable to ignore the affront to his scientific ability offered by Ward and Wallis, Hobbes replied in a revised edition of *De Corpore* the following year. In this edition he included an appendix aimed at teaching his Oxford opponents a lesson in manners as well as mathematics.[10] A furious paper war thus began, which was to last virtually until the year of Hobbes's death. It was Hobbes's misfortune that his adversaries were excellent mathematicians. Nor should we lose sight of the fact that their judgment of Hobbes's scientific achievements have also been those of posterity.

It has been difficult for students and specialists alike to understand why Hobbes allowed himself to become involved in such a futile controversy and one, moreover, in which he was at such an obvious disadvantage. His special greatness as a political philosopher lay in his ability to simultaneously generalize and particularize. He was able to develop an argument in a uniquely systematic and comprehensive way, while always seeming to have concrete, identifiable political situations in mind. The majestic sweep of his propositions might offend, but they placed his political writings — in contrast to, say, Milton's tracts — far above the level of contemporary polemics. But when Hobbes shifted from political to scientific studies, he was confronted with problems which were intractable, not to say insoluble. As a result he was no longer able to rely on the rational method which had formerly played such a key part in his thought. Hobbes failed to see his dilemma because he was caught between the criticism of his enemies and his own vaulting scientific aspirations. The vain glory of Don Quixote which Hobbes describes as a "gallant Madness" in his political writings now appeared in his own career, as he found himself "publicly injured by many of whom I took no notice, supposing that the humour would spend itself; but, seeing it last and grow higher in this writing I now answer, I thought it necessary to make of some of them ... an example" (EW, V, 455).

A similar vein of quixotry runs through Hobbes's controversy with Bishop Bramhall. In 1654, John Davys of Kidwelly who had obtained a manuscript copy of Hobbes's *"Of Liberty, and Necessity"* published it without Hobbes's consent and accompanied it with an inflammatory preface in which clerics were compared to tinkers who made more holes than they found in the consciences they tried to solder (EW, IV, 235). Hobbes's failure to make his disapproval of the project known apparently led Bramhall to publish a rejoinder entitled "A Defence of the True Liberty of Human Actions From Antecedent or Extrinsic Necessity." Hobbes could not resist writing a scathing reply, "Questions concerning Liberty, Necessity and Chance," in which he challenged every paragraph of

Bramhall's treatise. Bramhall returned to the attack not only with a lengthy "Castigations of Hobbes's Animadversions" but also with an appendix entitled "The Catching of Leviathan the Great Whale," one of the first of numerous works to charge the author of *Leviathan* with atheism, blasphemy, and impiety. The controversy was terminated only with Bramhall's death in 1663. It will suffice here to note that the end of this phase of Hobbes's quarrel with the clergy resulted in a standoff. Against Bramhall's Arminian arguments in favor of free will, Hobbes was able to gain at least a stalemate because of his dialectical skill and philosophical sophistication. On the other hand, the reputation which Bramhall's appendix aided in establishing for Hobbes was not a desirable one. During the Restoration, clerical forces would mount an extraordinary campaign against Hobbes's philosophy, focusing on *Leviathan* — the *monstrum horrendum* — as the main object of their vilification and ridicule.

Hobbes's clash with the Oxford mathematicians and with Bishop Bramhall did not prevent him from continuing his philosophical inquiries, but the results sometimes reflect his overriding preoccupation with controversial matters. A good example of Hobbes's loss of concentration is *De Homine* which was intended to complete his original philosophical design: De Corpore, De Homine, De Cive. Published in 1658, *De Homine* consisted mostly of chapters on optics which Hobbes had translated into Latin from his unpublished English treatise of 1646 (supra, p. 22). To this was added, with little evident connection, a short account of man's speech, appetites, and passions which, though significantly modified in some respects, was even briefer than his earlier versions of human nature in *The Elements of Law* and *Leviathan*.

Hobbes was spared at least one possible source of tribulation — the return of the Stuarts to England. The Protectorate came to an end in the events of 1658 and 1659. Oliver Cromwell died on September 3, 1658. By the end of May, 1659, his son and political heir Richard Cromwell had retired into private life. On May 29, 1660, Charles II landed in England. Any apprehensions that Hobbes may have had concerning his fate at the Restoration were quickly dispelled. In a striking anecdote, Aubrey relates that

about two or three dayes after his Majestie's happy returne, that, as He was passing in his coach through the Strand, Mr. Hobbes was standing at Little

Salisbury-house gate (where his Lord then lived). The King espied him, putt of his hatt very kindly to him, and asked him how he did. About a weeke after, he had orall conference with his Majesty at Mr. S. Cowper's, where, as he sate for his picture, he was diverted by Mr. Hobbes pleasant discourse. Here his Majestie's favours were redintegrated to him, and order was given that he should have free accesse to his Majesty. (152)

The king was "much delighted," both "in his witt" and in his character, and granted Hobbes a pension of one hundred pounds a year, a pension which seems to have been paid for a considerable length of time, even if not until the end of Hobbes's life.[11] The philosopher did not give up his independence when he received royal protection. In contrast to the fulsome panegyrics of the time, Hobbes's references to the King are quite restrained. Hobbes's frankness did not alienate the King who possessed the same qualities of wit and humor that Aubrey believed he appreciated in the philosopher: "The witts at Court were wont to bayte him. But he feared none of them, and would make his part good. The King would call him *the Beare:* Here comes the Beare to be bayted. . . . He was marvellous happy and ready in his replies, and that without rancor (except provoked)" (153). In 1668 the King did forbid the publication of Hobbes's *Behemoth,* a controversial history of the causes of the Civil War, but it was with an aim of protecting Hobbes's own interests.

The King's protection did not completely insure Hobbes from danger of persecution. After the Great Plague of 1665 and the Great Fire of 1666, the House of Commons established a committee "against Atheism and Profaneness," which was "empowered to receive information touching such books as tend to atheism, blasphemy and profaneness, or against the essence and attributes of God, and in particular the book published in the name of one White[12] and the book of Mr Hobbes called 'Leviathan' and to report the matter with their opinion to the House."[13] Although nothing seems to have come of this resolution, it may have aroused Hobbes's fears. Characteristically, his response was an inquiry into the actual state of the laws concerning heresy in England; the fruit of this inquiry was "An Historical Narration concerning Heresy and the Punishment thereof," which, however, was not published until after Hobbes's death. Because of the influence of the clergy with the Licensers, Hobbes was refused permission in 1668 to publish a new edition of *Leviathan* and in 1670, the Master of the Stationer's Company, accompanied by an armed escort, seized the sheets of a reprint of Hobbes's controversial work which were then being printed. Prevented from publishing *Leviathan* in England, Hobbes brought out a revised Latin translation in Amsterdam. In place of the original "Review and Conclusion," Hobbes inserted a defense of his theological propositions and a brief historical survey of heresy. Also suppressed were two original works of the year 1668: "Dialogue between a Philosopher and a Student of the Commons Laws of England" and a Latin metrical poem entitled "Historia Ecclesiastica." In the former Hobbes sought to controvert the encroachments of constitutional lawyers against the royal prerogative; in the latter those of clergymen upon the civil power.

The high point of attacks upon Hobbes's writings may have been the expulsion from Oxford in 1669 of a self-styled disciple, Daniel Scargil, for teaching theses from *Leviathan* subversive to the faith and morals of students. Scargil was made to participate in a public recantation in which he ascribed his erring ways to Hobbist principles. Five years later the Dean of Christ Church Oxford, Dr. John Fell — himself later immortalized in a satiric epigram — suppressed a tribute to Hobbes's character and learning and inserted various uncomplimentary passages in a Latin translation of Anthony Wood's *History and Antiquities*. Hobbes was granted permission from the King to reply in a dignified letter, addressed to Wood, but subsequently shown to Fell. Another note was appended to the book, in which Fell characterized Hobbes as "irritabile illud et vanissimum Malmesburiense animal,"[14] and pretended that the offending passages had been composed, not by himself or Wood but by Aubrey or Hobbes.

In depicting Hobbes in terms of such monstrosity and deformity, Fell suggests the lengths to which Hobbes's critics were prepared to go in order to exclude him from active participation in the intellectual life of the Restoration. Perhaps the clearest evidence of their success can be seen in Hobbes's relations with the scientists of the newly formed Royal Society. In 1662 when the Royal Society was officially constituted by a charter from the King, Hobbes was already seventy-four and had published his major work. Still in active correspondence with Parisian scientific circles, and enjoying royal favor, he certainly deserved a membership.

The Royal Society, however, had originated at Gresham College,

Oxford, during the Protectorate, and Hobbes's Oxford adversaries, Ward and Wallis, along with Robert Boyle, were determined, on both scientific and religious grounds, to prevent his admission. Hobbes presented numerous memoranda and demonstrations to the Royal Society, but was never accepted as a fellow. In truth, the group was not what one could call an illustrious assemblage of scientists; it included such virtuosi, antiquarians, and dilletantes as Devonshire, Aubrey, Samuel Pepys, John Evelyn, Dr. Walter Charleton, and John Dryden. Hobbes himself felt that the Royal Society was not fulfilling its proper function — the formulation of broad and far-reaching hypotheses on the science of nature. To combat the triviality of their experiments, Hobbes proposed that its members apply themselves to his own doctrine of motion to discover some of the "causes of natural events from them" (EW, IV, 437). Needless to say, neither of these proposals was ever acted upon.

Hobbes was indeed at heart a Don Quixote. He gave another notable example of naïveté in the year before his death. Isolated as he was from the scientific life of his times, Hobbes decided to return to his early humanistic interests, and at the age of eighty-nine published a complete, metrical translation of the *Iliad* and *Odyssey* to which he added a preface on the "virtues of the heroic poem." Although Hobbes had largely given up his philosophical pursuits, his explanation for undertaking such a vast project at such a late age shows that he had not lost his verve and spirit: "Why, then, did I write it? Because I had nothing else to do. Why publish it? Because I thought it might take off my adversaries from showing their folly upon my more serious writings, and set them upon my verse to their wisdom. But why without annotations. Because I had no hope to do it better than Mr. Ogilby" (EW, X, x).

Hobbes was fortunate that his health improved from forty onward when, according to Aubrey, he acquired "a fresh, ruddy complexion," but he nevertheless had several illnesses. In 1646 and 1668 Hobbes was at the point of death. Infirmities multiplied as he grew older. He suffered pain in his side, he was subject to unsteadiness in gait, and his hands became paralytical so that he was hardly able to write. "In the absence of his Amanuensis," writes Aubrey, "he made Scrawls on a piece of paper to remind him of the conceptions of his Mind he design'd to have committed to writing" (156). In spite of illness and age, however, Hobbes was able to remain mentally alert and active. He even tried to assist his natural longevity by self-administered therapy based upon the great principle of motion. Believing that "old men were drowned inwardly by their perspiration," Hobbes's remedy was to "walke up-hill and downe-hill in the parke, till he was in a great sweat, and then give the servant some money to rubbe him" (155). For the sake of his lungs, Hobbes sang aloud, though only "when he was abed and the dores made fast and was sure nobody heard him" (155). In later years Hobbes was studiously temperate in his diet, drinking no wine and eating fish rather than flesh. Yet Hobbes finally succumbed at age ninety-one to an illness on 9 December 1679 at the home of his master, the third Earl of Devonshire. Aubrey believed that "in the whole time of his sickness he was free from fever. He seemed therefor to dye rather for want of the Fuell of Life . . . then by the power of his disease" (159). It was reported that he died "in all the forms of a very good Christian."[15] He was buried at Hault Hucknall, beside the park of Hardwick Hall, and a black marble slab bears the simple Latin inscription "Vir probus et fama eruditionis domi forisque bene cognitus [An upright man and well-known at home and abroad for his learning]."

CHAPTER 2

# The Emerging Philosopher

I *Humanist History — Hobbes's Translation of Thucydides'*
History of the Peloponnesian War

HOBBES'S first published work, his version of Thucydides'
*History of the Peloponnesian War* in 1628–1629, merits careful attention even though it is a translation, because it espouses a
humanism which is seemingly quite different from the scientific
materialism of his later writings. Reflecting a humanistic preoccupation with political history and political institutions, it owes
its existence to a conviction that classical antiquity is the prime
source of political and historical wisdom. At the same time, it is inspired by a belief that the main task of the humanist scholar is the
education of the aristocracy in the service of the nation.

Hobbes's translation of Thucydides' *History* is accompanied by
an "Epistle Dedicatory," a preface and a "Life and History of
Thucydides." Perhaps the clearest evidence of Hobbes's humanist
concerns in his translation is to be found in the first of these prefatory sections. Though addressed to the second Earl of Devonshire,
"The Epistle Dedicatory" is written in memory of his father and
Hobbes's first master. The assumption underlying Hobbes's praise
of his former patron is that the responsibility of governing the
nation rests with members of the English upper class — "great persons" whose "worth" puts them above the vices of faction and
ambition (EW, VIII, iv). It is the duty of such persons to devote
their time and energy to the public good. In their actions they
should display the aristocratic virtues of "wisdom," "justice," and
"severity" to self and "magnanimity" to others (EW, VIII, iv). For
Hobbes as for earlier humanists, such actions are essentially heroic.
Disdaining a contemplative view of knowledge, any view which

32

regards learning as ornament, Hobbes regards the active life — "the management of great and weighty actions" — as the only legitimate end of the nobleman's education (EW, VIII, v). Not surprisingly, he finds in the life the first earl of Cavendish the perfect fulfillment of this educational ideal: "For his own study, it was bestowed, for the most part, in that kind of learning which best deserveth the pains and hours of great persons, history and civil knowledge: and directed not to the ostentation of his reading, but to the government of his life and the public good. For he read, so that the learning he took in by study, by judgment he digested, and converted into wisdom and ability to benefit his country" (EW, VIII, iv).

Hobbes came to this attitude toward learning from his humanist sympathies. The attitude was not a new one, having its roots in the sixteenth century, when the demand of the English nobility for practical training in civic affairs made it a basic part of Renaissance educational theory.[1] Behind this theory, moreover, is a conservative, hierarchical vision of society, a vision which is central to the argument of the "Epistle Dedicatory." Like many humanists, Hobbes was unable to conceive of a society without degree and order, without authority and submission. Hence he thinks that "ambition" in a member of the English upper class is a vice deserving of special condemnation (EW, VIII, iv). A considerable part of the dedication is devoted to praising Cavendish for preserving the traditional relationships between man and man in society: "No man better discerned of men: and therefore was he constant in his friendships, because he regarded not the *fortune* nor *adherence* but the *men*; with whom also he conversed with an openness of heart that had no other guard than his own integrity and that NIL CONSCIRE. To his equals he carried himself equally, and to his inferiors familiarly; but maintaining his respect fully, and only with the native splendour of his worth." (EW, VIII, iv–v).

This conception of society and of the proper place of the nobleman in it confers a sense of purpose to Hobbes's translation of Thucydides. Hobbes makes clear in the dedication that as a tutor he conceives his task to be the education of the young Cavendish in the values of his father. It was therefore entirely proper that Hobbes, the humanist scholar, should recommend Thucydides to his pupil: "I could recommend the author unto you, not impertinently, for that he had in his veins the blood of kings; but I choose rather to recommend him for his writings, as having in them profitable instruction for noblemen, and such as may come to have the management of great and weighty actions" (EW, VIII, v). Though Hobbes believes that the young Cavendish has at home "excellent ... examples and precepts of heroic virtue" he still commends the study of history because in it "actions of *honour* and *dishonour* do appear plainly and distinctly, which are which; but in the present age they are so disguised, that few there be, and those very careful, that be not grossly mistaken in them" (EW, VIII, vi). There is surely something Homeric in such a view of man in history, a view in which practical considerations are by no means effaced but in which history becomes an epic narrative, with man as a protagonist revealing in "great and weighty" actions heroic virtues which cannot but redound to the benefit of his country.

The humanist scholar believed that properly educated and inspired by good examples, aristocrats like Cavendish were capable of serving their nation well. For Hobbes, as for many humanists, the ancients were vastly superior to the moderns in aiding in this task: "It hath been noted by divers, that Homer in poesy, Aristotle in philosophy, Demosthenes in eloquence, and others of the ancients in other knowledge, do still maintain their primacy: none of them, exceeded, some not approached, by any in these later ages" (EW, VIII, vii). Of the branches of knowledge, history is the most valuable in Hobbes's opinion for the task of preparing the aristocrat for the conduct of politics. In his prefatory "To the Reader," Hobbes declares that "the principle and proper work of history" is "to instruct and enable men, by the knowledge of actions past, to bear themselves prudently in the present and providently towards the future" (EW, VII, vii). In this way, its aim is at once ethical and practical: to learn from the "lessons" of the past, not only how to avoid vice and follow virtue, but also how to follow the proper course of action in situations of conflicting interest.

In praising Thucydides as the classical historian best suited for this purpose, Hobbes makes history analogous to drama. In Hobbes's view, the reader is placed in a privileged position in Thucydides's *History,* as an omniscient "spectator" sitting "in the assemblies of the people and in the senate, at their debating; in the streets, at their seditions; and in the field, at their battles" (EW, VIII, viii). Digressions, lectures, precepts — these become interruptions in this "historical theater" where men are taught by action and example.

Despite his firm dedication to humanist values, the prefatory sections to Hobbes's translation of Thucydides' *History* depart from humanistic theory in one important respect. Though the use of historical narration for ethical teaching is of course a Renaissance practice, Hobbes differs from most Renaissance historians in his awareness that if history is to serve as a guide to politics, its writing must require a commitment to "Truth" and a disdain for the embellishments of rhetoric.[2] This concern makes Hobbes praise Thucydides for his choice of contemporary subject matter, his concern for factual accuracy, and his effort to trace causal connections between events (EW, VIII, xx–xxi). Indeed, much of the short "Life and History of Thucydides" is given over to a defense of the Athenian historian against the strictures of Dionysius Halicarnassus, a later Greek historian and teacher of oratory, for whom history was essentially a rhetorical genre closely allied to poetry. According to Hobbes, "in *truth* consisteth the *soul,* and in *elocution* the *body* of history. . . . the former without the latter, unapt to instruct" (EW, VIII, xx). If a reader is to benefit from such instruction, he must be able to "trace the drifts and counsels of the actors to their seat" (EW, VIII, viii).

It may be in Hobbes's dedication to truth that we can first detect the philosophical preoccupation of his later career. Combining veracity and eloquence gives history its identity for Hobbes and, at the same time, universalizes it. Universality depends upon a belief in the continuity of human history: the present and future will conform to the expectations raised in the reader by the past. The past is also accessible: the causes underlying political events are sufficiently manifest that by using reason an observer can discover the "lessons" which determine the course of politics and then apply these lessons in order to control the flow of events. There is a sense, however, in which Hobbes's faith in history might be seen as a precursor of his later scientific attitude. Hobbes's science of politics is infused with a moral didacticism of a particularly prudential kind and such a current may have passed from humanist history to humanist science conceived of as a genre concerned with man and society.[3] The fiercely rational outlook of *The Elements of Law, De Cive,* and *Leviathan* may not be entirely emancipated from the earlier tradition. When Hobbes turned from history to science for an explanation that would disclose the laws of politics, he replaced a faith in the value of observed examples with an equally strong faith in the internal mechanics of these examples.

## II    *Hobbes's Revaluation of History*

Hobbes's conversion to Euclid and geometry provides the starting point for a consideration of the change in attitude toward history that occurs in his later writings. In *The Elements of Law,* the first major philosophical work written after his discovery of Euclid, Hobbes describes past experience as "conjectural" (I, 4, 10),[4] and past knowledge as encrusted with error (I, 4, 10). Foresight (though not forethought or foreknowledge) becomes impossible, as history decomposes for Hobbes into a succession of distinct events without visible connection or continuity. In *Leviathan,* he declares that "the causes of good and evil fortune for the most part are invisible" to the observer (EW, III, 94), and the "chain of consequences" extended to such a length that "no human providence, is high enough, to give a man a prospect to the end" (EW, III, 356).

The implication of this change in attitude for Hobbes's faith in the benefits that accrue from the study of history is of course devastating, but his doubts went deeper than skepticism about the ethical function of history. What really separates his later outlook from the point of view of his translation of Thucydides' *History* is a healthy distrust of all existing knowledge — a distrust basic to the argument of *The Elements of Law, De Cive,* and *Leviathan.* In these works, reasoning and meditation replace "the authority of books" as the means to wisdom. Before men can even hope to achieve "true knowledge," they must "examine the definitions of former authors." Otherwise they will be led into "absurdities, which at last they see, but cannot avoid, without reckoning anew from the beginning" (EW, III, 24). The degree of Hobbes's own faith in the power of human reason is matched by the degree of his skepticism concerning the terms available in books for its encouragement. What is noteworthy in *Leviathan* is the intensity of Hobbes's sense of the inevitability of error bred by reliance upon authority (EW, III, 24).

In view of Hobbes's skepticism concerning history and existing learning, it is not surprising that he should do an about-face in his attitude toward classical historians. In *Leviathan,* Hobbes declared that "one of the most frequent causes" of rebellion against monarchy "is the reading of the books of policy, and histories of the ancient Greeks, and Romans; from which, young men, and all others that are unprovided of the antidote of solid reason, receiving a strong, and delightfull impression, of the great exploits of war, achieved by the conductors of their armies, receive withal a pleasing idea, of all they have done besides" (EW, III, 314–315). It was the "false Doctrine" engendered by such delightful impressions that Hobbes feared. To believe that "great prosperity" proceeded simply from "the vertue of their popular form of government" and that such explanations were true was "false doctrine". The emphasis of classical historians (though not Thucydides) upon the liberty enjoyed in popular commonwealths encouraged, in Hobbes opinion, just such a false doctrine which often had dangerous consequences: "From the same books, they that live under a monarch conceive an opinion, that the subjects in a popular commonwealth enjoy liberty; but that in a monarchy they are all slaves" (EW, III, 315).

Philosophy rather than history, reason rather than authority, logic rather than rhetoric, geometry rather than ethics, the moderns rather than the ancients — these were the distinctions on which Hobbes was to base his opposition to classical knowledge. In Hobbes's new view the achievements of every science are ultimately traceable to geometry: "For whatsoever assistance doth accrue to the life of man, whether from the observation of the heavens, or from the description of the earth, from the notation of times, or from the remotest experiments of navigation; finally, whatsoever things they are in which this present age doth differ from the rude simpleness of antiquity, we must acknowledge to be a debt which we owe merely to geometry" (EW, II, iv).

In spite of the drastic nature of this reversal in attitude, we can see here that Hobbes has not so much changed his old values as assimilated them within a new intellectual structure. For between the humanist scholar and the new philosopher there is at least one important point of agreement — that knowledge is practical and ethical, concerned above all with man in society. If the main source of knowledge to the early Hobbes is the historical *exempla,* then to the later Hobbes it is the geometrical axiom which serves as the model for a new approach to the "nature of right and wrong." The prefatory sections of Hobbes's translation of Thucydides and of *De Cive* each suggest in fact that the object of knowledge is to make "the actions of men" plainly and "distinctly known." Thus while Hobbes repudiated history as a guide for the conduct of politics, his new procedure was in no way incompatible with his earlier humanist aspirations. Even when Hobbes turned to mechanical philosophy, as in *A Short Tract on First Principles,* his attitude seemed to push his thought down paths that mechanical philosophers tended to shun.

### III   A Short Tract on First Principles

It seemed natural to Hobbes to appeal to geometry as the model for his philosophical explorations. He saw philosophy as "a way ... opened to us, in which we travel from the contemplation of particular things to the inference or result of universal actions" (EW, II, iii). Geometry was the best guide for this voyage, for geometry, Hobbes believed, was "the only science that it hath pleased God hitherto to bestow on mankind" (EW, III, 23–24). Geometry seemed to offer man a procedure more certain than the crude empiricism of history. *A Short Tract on First Principles* was the treatise in which Hobbes first attempted to apply the procedure of geometry to the search for truth. Unpublished in Hobbes's lifetime, *A Short Tract* was first discovered and given its title by Ferdinand Tönnies who suggested that it may have been composed as early as 1630, since in a letter of 1646, Hobbes wrote that what he had now completed on optics was derived from ideas he had put forward "about sixteen years since."[5] If *A Short Tract* was indeed written in 1630, well before the events which gave rise to Hobbes's later political writings, it provides a crucial test of the extent to which Hobbes's humanistic preoccupations survived in his scientific writings.

The model for *A Short Tract* is Euclid's *Elements. A Short Tract* consists of three sections, each of which is divided into "Principles" which Hobbes clearly takes to be self-evident and "Conclusions" which, though not obvious, are derived through a Euclidean process of deduction from the principles. In the first section Hobbes attempts to lay a basis for a mechanical philosophy of bodies in motion; in the second he develops the implications of this philosophy for a theory of light and optics; and in the third he makes his first attempt to construct a theory of human nature upon first principles. The affinity between Hobbes's procedure in this exercise and that of the New Philosophers is obvious. However, Hobbes retains two features which are characteristic of humanism as distinct from seventeenth century philosophy and science: (l) *A Short Tract* embraces a conception of genre that demands close imitation of a classical model; and (2) it aims to extend the formal procedures of geometry to human experience, which includes not only optics, but also psychology and ethics.

Central to the argument of *A Short Tract* is the proposition that "whatsoever moveth another, moveth it either by active power inherent in it self, or by motion received from another" (I, Princ. 9). The general topic was one which held a great fascination for Hobbes's contemporaries, motion being the most outstanding aspect of the researches of Galileo and Descartes in dynamics and of Harvey in biology. Some of the writers of the century had approached the subject with the desire to construct a metaphysical system or with a detached intellectual curiosity towards its manifestation in the observable phenomena in nature. Hobbes was not concerned either with pure metaphysics or pure observation, but with the practical possibility of inferring hidden causes from observed effects in areas which had always been subject to dispute and controversy. Hence, evidence in *A Short Tract* is entirely subservient to one aim: to give an account of optics, psychology, and ethics which is as rigorous as possible. Geometry acquires validity as a method only as it confers the certainty and prestige of mathematics.

The first and most obvious aspect of this geometry is the discarding of time, so important for Hobbes in his earlier preference for history. Indeed, in discussing principles and conclusions, Hobbes organizes his argument spatially: he often turns it into a Euclidean diagram and proceeds to describe the principles or conclusions themselves through their spatial relationships. Thus from the conclusion that "Nothing can move it self" (I, Conc. 10), Hobbes accounts for the motion of any body by the impact of another body external to it. The perfect symbol for this proposition is a straight line, since it is suggestive of the trajectory of a moving body. Hobbes defines "that which hath power to move" as an "Agent" (I, Princ. 3); conversely, he defines "that which hath power to be moved" as a "Patient" (I, Princ. 4). To describe movement that is imperceptible to the senses, Hobbes employs the term "locall motion" but even this motion implies the existence of two distinct bodies: "In Locall Motion, the Action of the Agent is the Locall Motion of the Patient" (I, Princ. 10). It is true that all motion implies time, but for Hobbes it is a time without content. Nowhere on his diagrams is there a place to measure velocity or force; as a result, his theory is restricted to problems in which time is not a factor.

Hobbes's spatial perspective, with its assumption that everything that is moved is moved by something else, is largely responsible for the difficulties he encounters in *A Short Tract*. In his theory of optics, Hobbes finds it necessary to introduce another element, "Species," to account for the impact of light upon distant objects: "Every Agent that worketh on a distant Patient, toucheth it, eyther by the Medium, or by somewhat issueing from it self, which thing so issueing lett be call'd Species" (II, Princ. I). From this account, it is apparent that for Hobbes, "Species" are a real projection, outward, of corporeal energies which are perceived in the mind by the "several 'Actions of External' things upon the Animal Spirits" (III, Conc. 3). But since they "are not in themselves entities," they are neither wholly describable nor wholly finite. Because they are not finite, they cannot, of course, be diminished: "Agents send out their species continually. For seeing the Agent hath power in it self to produce such species, and is alwayes applyed to the patient, which is somewhat in it self, it shall (by the 8 Concl. Sect. I) produce and send out species continually" (II, Conc. 5). "Species proceede infinitely" (II, Con. 6). This notion of "Species" poses a major difficulty for Hobbes. "If bodyes continually send out so many substantiall species, how can they exist without supply?" He admits that "this is indeed hard to determine" but goes on to suggest that "we may with probability imagine, that as Fyery bodyes, which send out most Species, are manifestly and sensibly supplyed with fuell: so other bodyes, sending out fewer, may have a supply of Nutriment, by converting other bodyes or Species adjacent, into themselves" (II, Conc. 8). In the end, however, Hobbes is driven to confess "though the way how this be done, as allmost all the wayes of Nature, be to us not so perceptible" (II, Conc. 8).

But even if Hobbes acknowledges the difficulties of his theory of bodies in motion, he does not turn away from its implications for man. The third section of *A Short Tract,* though very brief, describes the characteristics of sense perception, understanding, and desire. Sense perception is a direct result of "Species of the external object, supposed to be present" working on the "Animal Spirits," which Hobbes, following a venerable tradition, defines as "the Instruments of Sense and Motion" (III, Conc. 5). Understanding in *A Short Tract* is only a slight variation of this formula: it is "the Motion of the Animal Spirits, by the Action of the brayne, qualifyed with the active power of the externall object" (III, Conc. 6). In the absence of any account of memory or cognition, Hobbes's "qualified" renders the term understanding vague and imprecise. But this term as well as sense perception, vague as they are, represent no more than the groundwork of the third term — that is, the more fully developed treatment of desire which occupies the final pages of *A Short Tract*. The starting point of Hobbes's deductions is similar to that for sense perception and understanding — the existence of a subject that desires and an object external to this desire. Like sense perception and understanding, desire is essentially "a passive power": Hobbes describes "that which is desireable or good to one" as "that which hath power to attract" to it (III, Conc. 7). Conversely, aversion is "that which hath active power to repell it" (III, Conc. 7). An implicit parallelism in Hobbes's terminology supports this conception: "agent" and "patient" are related not only to the adjectives "active" and "passive" but also to "action" and "passion." An "agent" moves a "patient" by contact (an action moving a passion) and this results in an "accident."

Hobbes's conception of desire is rendered plausible through analogy. Its model is the lodestone, the very figure of attraction: "Though it may be doubted how the brayne can receive such power from the externall object; yet it is no more, nor otherwise, than when steele, touch'd by the Loadstone, receiveth from it a Magneticall virtue, to worke the same effects the Loadstone it self doeth" (III, Con. 4). The analogy implies that desire is essentially involuntary: one does not seek an object, one is drawn toward it. Against the well established priority that European philosophy had given to will, Hobbes wants to show that desires are independent of our conscious efforts. "Animal Spirits," he insists, "cannot be moved by will and Appetite; for these being facultyes, are but Accidents" (III, Conc. 2). To redress the balance that so favored volition, Hobbes omits any consideration of subordinate factors; significantly, the belief that general principles can be abstracted from the specific circumstances in which they appear to the human mind in everyday life was to become an important assumption of Hobbes's mature philosophy.

Equally significant in relation to Hobbes's later development is his ascription of the terms good and evil to the poles of attraction and aversion. In such an explanation, matters of right and wrong, which were traditionally accorded an objective status, now became subjective. But if desire is no longer measurable by standards beyond itself, the rigor of Hobbes's account makes desire seem at least logical and inevitable: "Appetite, as a power, is a passive power in the Animal Spirits, to be moved toward the object that moveth them" (III, Conc. 8). If this seems vaguely absolutist, it is with good reason. Hobbes's conception of good and evil, though profoundly at variance with that of traditional European thought, is no less universal; a universality no longer external but internal, in which the determining forces are located in the sympathies and antipathies of the mind. These forces are in and of the psyche, and if they are not disinterested they are at all times and in all places the same.

At first glance, this subjectivist explanation of good and evil seems to have much in common with many scientific treatises of the seventeenth century, for it is animated by pronounced determinist tendencies. Fiercely discontented with traditional learning, Hobbes is dedicated to a thoroughgoing mechanical explanation of natural phenomena. But while he shares the admiration of the new philosophy for mathematics, Hobbes does not achieve very much with his geometrical method. In *A Short Tract* he seems to move from principles to conclusions without passing through analysis.

As a scientific hypothesis, Hobbes's theory is unoriginal, unconvincing, and even backward. It attempts to offer a mechanical hypothesis to account for the action of one body on another at a distance; yet it is forced to revert to the humanist position, so repugnant to the mechanical philosopher, that "all the wayes of Nature, be to us not so perceptible." We should note as well that the analogy of the lodestone was among the traditional phenomena of "sympathy" and "antipathy." Hobbes's mechanical conception of bodies in motion appears in fact to be superimposed directly upon the "occult" conception of attraction.[6] It is true that, as J. W. N. Watkins has shown, the typically humanist theme of the natural hierarchy — the great chain of being — is missing from *A Short Tract*.[7] Yet, this theory is not always emphasized in the more fiercely realistic and pessimistic versions of Renaissance humanism. In its assertion of the concept of magnetic attraction, *A Short Tract* also incorporates another aspect of Renaissance scientific thought — a belief in the hidden power of natural agents.

Hobbes never published *A Short Tract,* and we may suppose that he became dissatisfied with the crudity of its formulations and the clumsiness of its terminology. Although the subjectivist account of good and evil presented here remains at the core of his ethics, it undergoes considerable amplification and refinement in his later works. Moreover, Hobbes discarded virtually all of the cumbersome scholastic terminology of this treatise. And yet *A Short Tract,* though hardly good enough to justify detailed commentary, is a significant portent. Its concern with ethics and its respect for geometry suggest some of his central interests; the problems which its exploratory nature inevitably entailed indicates the difficulties of evaluating the work of a philosopher as independent as Thomas Hobbes.

## CHAPTER 3

# The Elements of Law

*The Elements of Law, Natural and Politic,* which was circulated privately in manuscript in 1640, is the earliest and shortest version of Hobbes's mature philosophy. Although it was broken up into two distinct tracts entitled *Human Nature* and *De Corpore Politico,* which were brought out separately in 1650, it is a coherent and unified work. Hobbes's development as a philosopher in his later works can only be measured by examination of them against the background of *The Elements of Law.* The principle ideas of its second part were embodied in expanded form in *De Cive* (1642) and the outline of the whole can be detected in *Leviathan* (1650. Even the organization of *The Elements of Law* is preserved in these later works. Because it has been overshadowed by *Leviathan,* however, *The Elements of Law* was for a long time neglected and was not published in its original form until 1889.

Although the New Philosophy never entirely suppressed and eliminated Hobbes's earlier Humanism, it dominates his thought in *The Elements of Law.* Hobbes's philosophical solutions often seem fashioned for political problems, but his commitment to philosophy purges his treatise of any crudely polemical purpose. *The Elements of Law* represents his purest and most uncompromising attempt to extend the geometric analysis of natural phenomena to human nature and civil society. In the "Epistle Dedicatory," addressed to William Earl of Newcastle, Hobbes distinguishes between two kinds of learning, "mathematical and dogmatical": "The former is free from controversies and dispute, because it consisteth in comparing figures and motion only; in which things truth and the interest of men oppose not each other. But in the later [sic] there is nothing not disputable, because it compareth men, and meddleth with their right and profit; in which, as oft as reason is

44

against a man, so oft will a man be against reason. And from hence it cometh, that they that have written of justice and policy in general, do all invade each other, and themselves, with contradiction" (E.D., xv). Implicitly rejecting the latter, Hobbes proposes mathematics — specifically geometry — as a more rigorous model for the non-contradictory and non-controversial philosophy of "justice and policy" he desired. The function that Hobbes gives to mathematics is "to reduce this doctrine to the rules and infallibility of reason" (E.D., xv). This is the heart of his method. In place of the castles "in the air" of traditional moral philosophy, the analogy of an architectural structure with a solid foundation represents the movement of reason through various "degrees" of argument "till the whole be inexpugnable" (E.D., xv). Such a method is rigorously deductive; though it appeals to experience as confirmation of its axioms, it excludes "cases ... between sovereign and sovereign, or between sovereign and subject," which Hobbes says he will "leave to them that shall find leisure and encouragement thereto." It also has an adverse effect on his "style," which, says Hobbes, "is ... the worse, because I was forced to consult when I was writing, more with logic than with rhetoric" (E.D., xvi).

Hobbes's theoretical assumptions about method in *The Elements of Law* belong to the intellectual climate of its time. His basic approach is rationalistic. He believed that "what is proved by valid argument ... is believed by us whether we will or no" (LW, 5, 270). On this assumption deductive reasoning becomes effective. In *The Elements of Law,* as in *A Short Tract,* Hobbes used as his pattern Euclid's *Elements;* like the earlier treatise, *The Elements of Law* maintains a dispassionate attitude, with none of the emotional overtones of the later political works; its arrangement is a series of chapters containing propositions leading up to conclusions, each chapter having no other relation to the whole than as a stage in an interlocking sequence. It is divided into two parts, the first "Concerning men as persons natural" (*Human Nature*), the second "Concerning men as a body politic" (*De Corpore Politico*). The first part proceeds from an examination of men's cognitive faculties — sense perception, imagination, memory, and understanding — through a study of thought and speech to a view of what Hobbes calls "motive faculties" by which he means the pleasures and pains of the body, and the passions of the mind. The first part concludes with a consideration of "men in mere nature" accompanied by an examination of "natural laws" and of "the necessity and definition of the body politic." Proceeding from this foundation, the second part begins with the "generation" of civil society and moves through a comparison of the various kinds of government to an examination of the "causes of rebellion" and "duties of the sovereign." It concludes with a chapter on "the nature and kinds of laws." The insistence throughout upon continuity, simplicity, and purity corresponds to the mathematician's preoccupation with numerical pattern. The organization of *The Elements of Law* into multiples of ten — twenty chapters in the first part, ten in the second — stresses the mathematical coherence of the work and, incidentally, reminds us that this coherence is more than utilitarian.

## I   Human Nature

*Human Nature,* the first part of *The Elements of Law,* has been regarded by some critics as Hobbes's finest work. James Harrington viewed it as one of the "greatest of new lights," Joseph Addison considered it the "best of all his works," and Denis Diderot recommended its use as a textbook in schools.[1] Part of its interest stems from the fact that it is Hobbes's longest discourse on man; the comparable chapters in *Leviathan* are abbreviated, and the section on human nature in *De Homine* is reduced still further.

### 1.   *The Mental Faculties*

After a short introductory chapter devoted to definitions, Hobbes proceeds in the next two chapters to discuss man's mental faculties, dealing first with the senses, then with imagination, memory, and dreams. This part of *Human Nature* covers some of the same ideas as the second section of *A Short Tract,* but Hobbes discards much of the terminology of the earlier work. In particular, he dismisses the notion of "species visible and invisible ... passing to and fro from the object" as "worse than any paradox, as being a plain impossibility" (I, 2, 4). Like Galileo and Descartes, Hobbes now argues that "an image or colour" exists in our minds not in physical bodies, though Hobbes makes no attempt to explain how this phenomena is caused. As evidence, he cites the distorted reflection of "the sun and other visible objects ... in the water and in glasses," and the ability of some men to see the same object double (I, 2, 5). This emphasis upon optical illusion inevitably raises a doubt about our senses. If an object is not always what we perceive it to be, how far can our senses be trusted?

Not very far appears to be Hobbes's answer. His new terminology refers to sense impressions as "seemings" and "apparitions": "whatsoever accidents or qualities our senses make us think there be in the world, they are not there, but are seemings and apparitions only" (I, 2, 10). Hobbes's conclusion here is similar to that of Descartes who also held that the senses are not to be trusted, since they sometimes deceive.[2] Unlike Descartes, however, Hobbes was unwilling to fall back on the conviction that God, who has been proven to exist and who does not deceive, would not allow us to be deceived. Hence, Hobbes is unwilling to explain away the phenomena of natural deception. For him, man dwells in a world of appearances, his apprehensions frequently confused and obscure.

Yet, Hobbes never doubted that objects do in fact exist. Moreover, "the great deception of sense" can "by sense" be corrected, though not without a considerable effort (I, 2, 10). This correction does not take place when one sees "directly"; it occurs, on the contrary, when one sees "by reflection" — that is, by the refraction of an object in another medium or by its reflection mirrored on another surface, — "that colour is not in the object" (I, 2, 10).

A comparable conviction of the deficiency of our mental faculties is evident in Hobbes's treatment of memory, imagination, and dreams in chapter three. The spatial metaphor of standing water, stirred by the fall of a stone or wind into a motion which continues after the stone settles or the wind subsides, represents memory as the result of a physical movement that is always subsiding, always returning to an elemental stillness. In a more direct metaphor, Hobbes describes "remembrance" as "by little and little decaying" (I, 3, 1). The present participle makes it clear that memory is a process of forgetting which is always taking place. This factor is important because the act of remembering is for Hobbes more than a passive state. There is an essential distinction between "imagination," defined here as a "conception remaining ... after the act of sense" — which is a purely reflexive act of motion — and "remembrance" — which assumes a certain activity or at least a certain orientation of the faculties by which we "take notice of some or other of our conceptions." In fact, the latter faculty is so important that Hobbes calls it a "sixth sense" (I, 3, 6).

The transitory character of memories is not, however, their only deficiency. During man's waking hours, memories are obscure, their brightness dimmed by the vivacity of fresh "apparitions" (I, 3, 1). It is only in dreams that memories are restored to anything like their original strength and clarity. Yet dreams are a prime source of error. In the abeyance of reason, dreams present "the disorder and causal consequence of one image to another" (I, 3, 3) — a disorder which gives birth to "castles in the air, chimeras, and other monsters which are not in *rerum natura,* but have been conceived by the sense in pieces at several times" (I, 3, 4). The sheer intensity of such dreams provides another source of deception in their hallucinatory resemblance to waking life. As a result, "man can never know he dreameth:" "he may dream he doubteth, whether it be a DREAM or no; but the clearness of the imagination representeth every thing with as many parts as doth sense itself, and consequently, he can take notice of nothing but as present; whereas to think he dreameth, is to think those his conceptions past, that is to say, obscurer than they were in the sense: so that he must think them both as clear, and not as clear as sense, which is impossible" (I, 3, 8). At this point, Hobbes is unable even to suggest a criterion for distinguishing between dreams and reality and therefore is not surprised to hear a man "sometimes to tell his dream for a truth, or to take it for a vision" (I, 3, 10).

Hobbes's account of the mental faculties in these chapters has much in common with the rationalized universe of seventeenth century science. To our ingrained bias in favor of what is given to us in experience — it opposes the view that the senses deceive, that memory is unreliable, that waking and dreaming cannot be distinguished with certainty. To our prejudice for what is directly perceived and felt — it opposes the notion that sense impressions yield a "subjective" reality that can only be understood by a mechanistic hypothesis of bodies in motion. Yet in spite of his commitment to the dichotomy that exists between what appears and what is inferred, Hobbes rarely invokes this hypothesis for the purpose of causal explanation in his discussion of the human mind. Like many new philosophers, Hobbes proves his scientific orthodoxy with a nod toward mechanistic materialism; but his psychology offers little more than such a gesture as evidence that sense impressions, memories and dreams are the result of bodies in motion. Indeed the main emphasis of Hobbes's account is directed not toward causes but effects. An explanation of these effects is afforded by the

obvious moral implication which is present throughout *The Elements of Law:* man may so live as to use his mental faculties properly; on the other hand, he may, by failing to recognize their limitations, become a self-deceiving enthusiast whose energies on behalf
of his private truth prove a danger to civil society.

## 2.  *Thought, Language, and Speech*

At this point, Hobbes is confronted with a basic problem. If our
conceptions are so much more obscure than our sense impressions,
which in themselves are unreliable, how is it possible for us to order
these conceptions rationally? Hobbes's answer in chapter four is at
first not very promising: "The cause of the coherence or consequence of one conception to another, is their first coherence or
consequence at the time when they were produced by sense" (I, 4,
2). Such coherence amounts to little more than a rudimentary version of the associational psychology developed more fully by later
English empiricists.

Inadequate as this explanation is, however, it does not prevent
Hobbes from going on to give a more sophisticated account of
what he calls "discursion." Characteristically, Hobbes invokes the
spatial metaphor of a field to represent the topography of the
mind. To describe the mental process by which the individual
moves from one concept to another, he resorts to an animal image
— that of the hunting dog. Far from regarding mental activity as a
mechanical operation governed by the internal laws of motion,
Hobbes treats it as a vital but virtually instinctive process governed
by desire. The field over which the dog moves becomes the apt
metaphor for the mind's largely unconscious capacity for retrieval
and recovery. For Hobbes, this capacity takes three forms:
"ranging ... the hounds casting about at a fault in hunting" (I, 4,
3); "hunting or tracing ... as dogs trace after the beast by the smell
... or as men hunt after riches, place or knowledge" (I, 4, 4); and
"reminiscence," which Hobbes describes by the spatial analogy of
a search for a lost object: "the appetite to recover something lost,
proceeding from the present backward, from the thought of the
place where we miss it, to the thought of the place from whence we
came last; and from the thought of that, to the thought of the place
before, till we have in our mind some place, where we had the thing
we miss" (I, 4, 5).

The interrelationship of mind and body, so evident here, is one of Hobbes's leading themes. It accounts for his assumption that man is distinguished from beasts, not through his capacity for thought, which is instinctive, but through his capacity for language, which Hobbes describes in chapter five as necessary for the support of man's faulty memory:

> The experience we have hereof, is in such brute beasts, which, having the providence to hide the remains and superfluity of their meat, do nevertheless want the remembrance of the place where they hid it, and thereby make no benefit thereof in their hunger. But man who in this point beginneth to advance himself above the nature of beasts, hath observed and remembered the cause of this defect, and to amend the same, hath imagined and devised to set up a visible or other sensible mark, the which when we seeth again, may bring to his mind the thought he had when he set it up. (I, 5, 1).

Memory, we should note, is conceived in terms of the sense of sight. Because it is of a spatial rather than a temporal order, marks are defined as signposts which indicate places to which one intends to return or, conversely, around which one seeks to detour. "As men that have passed by a rock at sea," writes Hobbes, "set up some mark, whereby to remember their former danger, and avoid it" (I, 5, 1).

It is man's ability to give names to these marks that is the beginning of science, defined here in the broadest possible way. By naming and numbering things, man confers order on what in the life of brutes is irrational and random: "as a beast misseth not one or two out of her many young ones, for want of those names of order, one, two, three & c., which we call number; so neither would a man, without repeating orally, or mentally, the words of number, know how many pieces of money or other things lie before him" (I, 5, 4).

This contrast between memory and forgetfulness, order and chance, exemplifies the intimate connection between Hobbes's theory of mind and his theory of language. Because the senses are unreliable and memory is decaying, the names which man gives to his marks must be subject to unremitting scrutiny. To prevent human beings from degenerating to the level of beasts, Hobbes calls for the repeated renewal of words by direct contact with the specific tangible conceptions they represent.

Thus language is not autonomous for Hobbes. Rather it is under permanent subjection, so that words must be coextensive with the thoughts they represent, and the truth of any statement is made to depend upon its congruity with images. Conversely, error arises from the separation of words from conceptions. We achieve "understanding" by finding out "the true meaning of what is said." It follows that for Hobbes a prime source of intellectual confusion is "equivocation of names." So great, in fact, is the temptation for man to err in this respect that "there is scarce any word that is not made equivocal by divers contextures of speech, or by diversity of pronunciation and gesture" (I, 5, 7).

Man's propensity toward intellectual confusion combined with the unreliability of his senses accounts for the errors of past thinkers:

Now if we consider the power of those deceptions of sense, mentioned in chapter 2 section 10, and also how unconstantly names have been settled, and how subject they are to equivocation, and how diversified by passion, (scarce two men agreeing what is to be called good, and what evil; what liberality, what prodigality; what valour, what temerity) and how subject men are to paralogism or fallacy in reasoning, I may in a manner conclude, that it is impossible to rectify so many errors of one man, as must needs proceed from those causes. (I, 5, 14)

Here again we can observe how Hobbes's ideas are motivated by a humanist imperative; like the New Philosopher, Hobbes uses this pessimistic judgment concerning the errors of past thinkers as a platform on which to call for renewal of knowledge through reason, but the objects of this knowledge are social values, not natural entities.

In chapter six Hobbes seeks to define knowledge more precisely and to distinguish it from belief and opinion. Because of the unreliability of both sense impressions and words, Hobbes's discussion of knowledge and opinion does not altogether exclude the possibility of a radical skepticism. Belief, which Hobbes defines as "the admitting of propositions upon trust" (I, 6, 9), and conscience, which he terms "opinion of evidence" (I, 6, 8), are clearly inferior to "perfect and manifest knowledge." Although Hobbes stresses the conviction that belief "in many cases is no less free from doubt, than perfect and manifest knowledge" (I, 6, 9), there are obviously many beliefs in Hobbes's opinion which are not immune to doubt.

Experience offers no solution because its "signs" are "conjectural" and by its self it "concludeth nothing universally" (I, 4, 10). But since Hobbes's political theory rests on the premise that experience teaches us what things are beneficial or harmful to us, he is not willing to avow the unreliability of experience. In this chapter, Hobbes distinguishes between two kinds of knowledge — "original" knowledge and knowledge of "the truth of propositions" (I, 6, 1). The former is shared by both man and beast and leads to prudence; its intellectual product is history. The latter is the province of man alone and leads to wisdom; its intellectual product is science. Both forms are derived from experience. Rejecting any view of reason that regards reason as powerless and unable to reach the stable and universal truth, Hobbes assimilates knowledge to experience. Like Descartes, he conceives of philosophy as the personal task of the philosopher. Right reason becomes reasoning. He stipulates an exact correspondence between "man's conceptions and the words that signify such conceptions in the act of ratiocination" (I, 6, 3).

The quality of mental activity is thus Hobbes's final test of knowledge. An act of cognition is at the same time an act of perception, and each word that refers to a conception must also refer to the "thing that produced the same by our senses" (I, 6, 4). To these two steps in the chain of reasoning Hobbes adds two further steps: "the third is, that we have joined the names in such manner, as to make true propositions; the fourth and last is, that we have joined those propositions in such a manner as they be concluding" (I, 6, 4). It is this unified and wholly sustained act of reasoning that Hobbes opposes to belief and conscience — both of which depend upon our willingness to accept ideas without actually thinking them through for ourselves.

The close relationship between words and thoughts in Hobbes's account of reasoning shows that *The Elements of Law* implicitly assumes the fundamental ontological postulate of Hobbes's metaphysical speculations: the assimilation of spirit to matter, of mind to body. The processes and properties of both the physical world and human consciousness are subject to the laws that govern the universe and can be explained, at least in theory, in terms of bodies in motion. Hobbes's position concerning the unity of body and mind is connected to his position that reason cannot and should not function independently of the senses, even though the senses may be subject to error. The possibility that he might be dreaming, deceived by his senses, or suffering from a faulty memory obviously seems insufficient to Hobbes to cast doubt on the validity of his reasoning. It is the belief that the mind possesses the power to plunge beneath the "apparitions" and "seemings" in order to discover the laws that govern man and society that provides the key to Hobbes's release from skepticism.

### 3. *Psychology and Ethics*

Since reasoning is governed by desire, the problem of knowledge is closely linked to the problem of value which, as we have seen, Hobbes equated with desire in *A Short Tract*. At first, the seventh chapter of *The Elements of Law* appears merely to be a restatement of Hobbes's "brutal" subjectivist ethics, his initial, stark identification of good and evil with attraction and repulsion: "This motion, in which consisteth pleasure or pain, is also a solicitation or provocation either to draw near to the thing that pleaseth, or to retire from the thing that displeaseth" (I, 7, 2). But this view is considerably modified during the course of the chapter. Hobbes begins by insisting that some ends can become transformed into means to further ends. In this way, he introduces the idea of a chain of desires which, once started, tends to extend itself almost indefinitely; one desire leads on naturally to the next. Moreover, Hobbes assumes that a chain of desires presupposes an awareness of an eventual end when the object is achieved; for Hobbes, that end is an illusion. His attitude is perhaps best summed in his celebrated rejection of the philosopher's *summum bonum:* "But for an utmost end, in which the ancient philosophers have placed felicity, and have disputed much concerning the way thereto, there is no such thing in this world, nor way to it, more than to Utopia: for while we live, we have desires, and desire presupposeth a farther end" (I, 7, 6).

Hobbes's view of human nature still assumes the existence of specific desires: man is invariably self-conscious in identifying and pursuing them. But he now emphasizes that these states of desire are never fulfilled or exhausted.[3] Indeed it is the very act of desiring, not the end, that gives man pleasure: "Felicity, therefore (by which we mean continual delight), consisteth not in having prospered, but in prospering" (I, 7, 7). Beyond the horizon of any single object attained, there is thus always a further horizon.

The emphasis that Hobbes places upon the satisfactions that come from activity, in contrast to merely passive enjoyment, is confirmed by his distinction, in chapter eight, between "pleasures of sense" and "pleasures of the mind." Pleasures of the sense are by their very nature neglectful of the future, forgetful of the past; they "please only for the present, and taketh away the inclination to observe such things as conduce to honour; and consequently maketh men less curious, and less ambitious, whereby they less consider the way either to knowledge or to other power" (I, 10, 3). By contrast, pleasures of the mind, which include knowledge, riches, place of authority, friends, favors or good fortune (I, 8, 4) are acquired. Thus, they are desires we hope to obtain in the future and presuppose "a remembrance of what is past" and a knowledge of "something at the present that hath power to produce it" (I, 8, 3). While Hobbes is ostensibly neutral toward these two different kinds of desire, he describes "dullness" as the consequence of being "addicted to ease, food, onerations and exonerations of the body" (I, 10, 3).

The pleasures of sense are not in fact an important factor in Hobbes's account of human nature; his treatment of them is perfunctory and unoriginal. A consequence of this attitude is that power, defined as the capacity to produce something in the future, becomes the main focus of his attention, directly or indirectly, in chapters eight through twelve. As a spring of action, power comes to include: (1) the faculties of mind and body; (2) riches, place of authority, friendship, etc.; and (3) excess of power of one man over another.[4] Such an emphasis naturally puts a premium on reputation, prestige, status, and it is not surprising to find out that "Honour" — defined as "the acknowledgment of power" — occupies a central position in Hobbes's theory of human nature. A legacy of his humanism is that his treatment of "Honour" in chapter eight is cast largely in aristocratic, heroic terms (I, 8, 5). The "value of worth" which Hobbes invokes here as synonyms for "Honour" are achieved by such "powers" as those which made Hobbes, in his dedication to his translation of Thucydides' *History,* regard the first Earl of Devonshire as a person of "worth." Even though he refrains from identifying the signs of honor with a particular class, they are such as we might well expect an obedient subject of the seventeenth century monarchies to admire, worship, or venerate.

To account for the role of power in human affairs, Hobbes devoted chapter nine to a theory of the passions. In composing this chapter, Hobbes may have drawn, not only upon Aristotle's *Rhetoric,* as Leo Strauss has shown,[5] but also upon numerous Renaissance treatises on the passions, such as Peter de la Primaudaye's *French Academy* or Nicholas Coëffeteau's *Table of Human Passions.*[6] Significantly, there is little interest in Hobbes's treatment in the outward "expression" of the passions by bodily gestures or features. Instead, he attempts to define the passions largely through an appeal to "our imagination or conception" of the relation of our power to the power of others. Central to this awareness is an interior emotion of the mind different from the passions which are visible to others. Ethically, this inner emotion is of greater import than the external passions, since it is against it that the charge that Hobbes is a psychological egoist is usually directed. Thus laughter "is nothing else but a sudden glory arising from sudden conception of some eminency in ourselves, by comparison with the infirmities of others" (I, 9, 13). Charity is "an argument to a man of his own power ... to find himself able, not only to accomplish his own desires, but also to assist other men in theirs" (I, 9, 17). Lust is briefly treated; Hobbes emphasizes that "the delight men take in delighting, is not sensual, but a pleasure or joy of the mind, consisting in the imagination of the power they have so much to please" (I, 9, 15).

Of all the passions, the most important for Hobbes in *The Elements of Law* is joy or glory, which he defines as "the internal gloriation or triumph of the mind" (I, 9, 1). Though Hobbes affirms that this inner glory may be grounded on an "assured and certain experience of our own actions," the main emphasis of his treatment of glory in *The Elements of Law* falls upon its illusory aspects. The possibility that "one may think well of himself, and yet be deceived" is called "false glory" (I, 9, 1). An even more serious source of delusion is "vain glory," which induces the quiescence of a dreamworld cut off from "appetite" or "endeavour": "the fiction (which also is imagination) of actions done by ourselves, which never were done, is glorying; but because it begetteth no appetite nor endeavour to any further attempt, it is merely vain and unprofitable; as when a man imagineth himself to do the actions whereof he readeth in some romant, or to be like unto some other man whose acts he admireth" (I, 9, 1).

Hobbes uses his distinction between a "just" and a "vain" perception of our power in relation to the power of others as a criterion for distinguishing between madness and sanity in chapter ten. For Hobbes, madness begins at the point where man's relationship to power is ruptured. According to the different ways this rupture occurs, there will be different forms of madness. One form is "vain dejection," which consists of the "fear of the power, without any other sign of the act to follow" (I, 9, 2); Hobbes cites as an example those "melancholy men that have imagined themselves as brittle as glass, or have some other like imagination" (I, 10, 11). The opposite of "vain dejection" is "vain glory"; among his examples of "vain glory," Hobbes lays particular stress upon Don Quixote (I, 10, 9).

Chapter eleven, on God, is a kind of appendix to the discussion of power in chapters nine and ten. This chapter is not foreshadowed and seems slightly out of place in Hobbes's argument, but he tries to fit it in by recasting a traditional causal argument for the existence of God in terms of his previous discussion: "For the effects we acknowledge naturally, do necessarily include a power of their producing, before they were produced; and that power presupposeth something existent that hath such power; and the thing so existing with power to produce, if it were not eternal, must needs have been produced by somewhat before it, and that again by something else before it; till we come to an eternal, that is to say, to the first power of all powers, and first cause of all causes. And this is it which all men call by the name of God" (I, 11, 2). The inadequacy of Hobbes's theology here seems glaringly apparent. What is an object of rational knowledge is God taken as the first cause among causes, the highest power among powers. In short, the essence of the Hobbesian deity is largely determined by his philosophical purpose which is to sustain the social order as Hobbes conceives of it. Now it is quite true that God is all-powerful, but a God whose very essence is power is obviously insufficient as an object of religious faith, as the following passage indicates: "To honour God internally in the heart, is the same thing with that we ordinarily call honour amongst men: for it is nothing but the acknowledging of his power; and the signs thereof the same with the signs of the honour due to our superiors, mentioned chapt. 8, sect. 6 (viz): to praise, to magnify, to bless him" (I, 11, 12). In spite of Hobbes's attempt to integrate his discussion of religion with his earlier argument, he must have been unsatisfied with his treatment of the subject. In subsequent works, he revised and expanded the chapters on religion more than any other part of his philosophy.

In chapter twelve, Hobbes returns to the main line of his argument with an analysis of deliberation and will. Hobbes's emphasis upon the "pleasures of the mind" rather than the "pleasures of sense" leads him to acknowledge the fact that human beings perform many actions with deliberation. But Hobbes goes on nevertheless to define deliberation in terms of desires and aversions. Thus, the deliberation of an action requires two conditions: "that it be future" and "that there be hope of doing it, or possibility of not doing it" (I, 12, 2). Once an end is decided upon, deliberation follows a rigorously logical pattern. Characteristically, in deliberating a man alternates between "appetite and fear" until the action be either done or some accident" brings the sequence to an end (I, 12, 1). In this pattern, will becomes "the last appetite of deliberation" (I, 12, 2). Since will is subsumed under desire, choice, as we customarily think of it, becomes impossible. Inasmuch as a person is totally committed to his desire, he is precluded from becoming involved in a situation where he must, for instance, decide between what morality dictates and the satisfactions of his desire. Further, Hobbes's deliberation is confined to "the pleasures of the mind" — future desires. To an explanation of "pleasures of the sense," it contributes nothing. These exist, presumably, in an undifferentiated present in which the requirements of prudence do not apply. In dramatic terms, deliberation is experienced as a succession of reversals between the polar opposites of appetite and fear, rather than as a sustained conflict between opposing courses of action. A character who embodies such a pattern is much more likely to seem comically indecisive than tragically involved.

This sort of psychology, simplifying desire and will to a conflict between "appetite" and "fear," appears to best advantage in Hobbes's analysis of situations of last resort. A central element in Hobbes's political theory, the fear of death, provides the most vivid and concrete examples in *The Elements of Law:* the prisoner who, though brought to prison against his will, "yet goeth upright voluntarily, for fear of being trailed along the ground," or the man "who throweth his goods out of a ship into the sea, to save his person" (I, 12, 3). These examples refer to circumstances of extreme danger, circumstances in which the mind discovers the difference between voluntary and involuntary actions in the very paucity of choices confronting it. Insofar as voluntary action is an intensification of the desire for self-preservation, Hobbes suggests a plausible way of explaining how will can be viewed as "the last appetite of deliberation."

## 4.  Man's Natural State

After a short chapter in which he returns to the theme of the "epistle dedicatory" — the distinction between dogmatic opinion and mathematical demonstration — Hobbes declares that he has completed his account of "the whole nature of man, consisting in the powers natural of his body and mind" (I, 14, 1). He is now ready to consider "in what estate of security this our nature hath placed us, and what probability it hath left us of continuing and preserving ourselves against the violence of another" (I, 14, 2). Hobbes then goes on in chapter fourteen to formulate his famous view that the state of nature is a state of war. That the term "state of nature" was not a fundamental part of his thinking might be concluded from his failure to employ it in *The Elements of Law.* This term seems to have been suggested by the phrase, "by nature," which refers to a condition existing prior to the formation of society.

Hobbes offers several reasons why such a condition must be viewed as a state of war: some men are "vainly glorious, and hope for precedency and superiority above their fellows" (I, 14, 3); all men "by natural passion are by divers ways offensive one to another" (I, 14, 4); and "many men's appetites carry them to one and the same end; which end sometimes can neither be enjoyed in common, nor divided" (I, 14, 5). In these circumstances fear is inevitable; it becomes a generalized awareness of danger, a mutual awareness that presupposes a disharmony between the self and others. Even those who are "moderate and look for no more but equality of nature shall be obnoxious to the force of others" (I, 14, 3). At this point, Hobbes seems well on the way to viewing man's natural state as a simple deduction from his analysis of human nature and human passions. Nonetheless Hobbes is willing to identify it with actual historical conditions, chiefly as a way of making it comprehensible to readers: "(as we know also that it is, both by the experience of savage nations that live at this day, and by the histories of our ancestors, the old inhabitants of Germany and other now civil countries, where we find the people few and short lived, and without the ornaments and comforts of life, which by peace and society are usually invented and procured)" (I, 14, 12).

Inevitably, a consideration of man's natural state brings about a reconsideration of society. Once human relationships are no longer regarded as based upon trust, the traditional model of society as a natural hierarchy becomes void. In his translation of Thucydides' *History* Hobbes assumed, as we have seen, the classical and humanist model of nature as a great chain of being. *The Elements of Law* projects a quite different idea: the modern conception of nature as a democracy of beings. This conception is compatible with a view of society as an artificial hierarchy; for this natural democracy, as Hobbes envisages it, is based not upon an equality of talents but upon a rough and somewhat paradoxical equality of powers. Its starting point is fear: a recognition of the fact that there is no way in which anyone by himself can protect his body from a sudden, unpremeditated assault by another person. Fear is the agonizing awareness that the individual who in Hobbes's words "is the weaker in strength and wit, or in both, may utterly destroy the power of the stronger, since there needeth but little force to the taking away of a man's life" (I, 14, 2).

If an awareness of man's natural state is a dangerous, even intimidating, experience — one that excludes reassuring emotions, a sense of well being, and complacency — it is also, fortunately, an experience from which we can learn. It does give us guidance. It teaches us, for instance, that it is "not against reason that a man doth all he can to preserve his own body and limbs, from both death and injury." And since "that which is not against reason, men call right," the desire for self-preservation becomes "a *right of nature*" (I, 14, 6). From this experience, Hobbes goes on to adduce three additional "rights of nature." The first is man's right "to use all means and do whatsoever action is necessary for the preservation of his body" (I, 14, 7); the second is his right to be "judge himself of the necessity of the means and the greatness of the danger" (I, 14, 8). The third is that man "hath right to all things, that is to say, to do whatsoever he listeth to whom he listeth, to possess, use, and enjoy all things he will and can" (I, 14, 10). To exercise these three rights, however, is to ensure conflict: man's natural state is dangerous, for "no man is of might sufficient to assure himself for any long time, of preserving himself thereby" (I, 14, 14). From this fact, the most important deduction follows: "reason ... dictateth to every man for his own good, to seek after peace, as far forth as there is hope to attain the same" (I, 14, 14).

This argument provides a very clear indication of the way in which the passion of fear comes, in Hobbes's analysis, to support reason. To submit to reason is to submit to the exigencies of man's natural state, and it does not exclude at least one passion, that of fear, although reason still possesses a normative character. Reason still dictates the rules by which men ought to behave—rules which Hobbes, following a long tradition, terms the laws of nature. The next three chapters take us straight from a consideration of the rights of nature to an examination of the laws of nature.

## 5.  The Laws of Nature

The theory of natural law which Hobbes sets forth in chapters fifteen through eighteen is based upon his view that the laws of nature must not only be demonstrated with rigor but also be shown to conform to experience. If the laws of nature are to be demonstrated with rigor, they must depend *not* upon will — the consent of "nations" or even of all mankind — but upon reason. Whereas will is susceptible to error induced by evil customs or violent passions, reason — free from custom and from all passions save fear — is therefore free from error. If the laws of nature are to conform to experience, they must conform to the assumption that reason is prudential in that it directs every man to seek his own good which for Hobbes is synonymous with self-preservation. It follows obviously and immediately in Hobbes's view that "there can be no other law of nature than reason, nor no other precepts of NATURAL LAW, than those which declare unto us the ways of peace, where the same may be obtained, and of defence where it may not" (I, 15, 1).

Hobbes's emphasis upon the prudential character of reason at this point might seem incompatible with his ethical ideal. Why must the desire of individuals to seek their own good always coincide with the common desire for peace? To answer this question, we must take note of Hobbes's assumptions about two crucial terms — "good" and "reason." The relation of the two terms to each other could scarcely be closer. As we have seen, Hobbes identifies good with appetite and evil with aversion: whatever is the object of a man's appetite is good and whatever is the object of his aversion is evil. Good and evil therefore appear to be relative notions, susceptible to subjective interpretation. But Hobbes also assumes that present desires and fears can be converted from ends into means to future ends. Implicit in the statement that every man desires his own good appears to be the assumption that fear has converted "good" from present satisfactions to future ends.[7] Support for this view of "good" is afforded by Hobbes's conception of reason. In spite of his egalitarian view of the body, his view of the mind is hierarchical, preserving the distinction, cherished by humanists, between the rational and the irrational. Thus Hobbes echoes the traditional view that praises cool reason at the expense of violent passions, mind over body, choice over impulse, future good over present gratification. Since "reason . . . is the same in all men, because all men agree in the will to be directed and governed in the way to that which they desire to attain, namely their own good, which is the work of reason" (I, 15, 1), laws of nature that are based upon reason acquire universal validity. Only in this way can the individual desire for self-preservation be transformed into the common good — not just one man, but all men desire peace.

In spite of its prudential nature, reason then is still a regulative, normative principle in Hobbes's theory of human behavior. The laws of nature are laws which describe, not how we actually act, but how we must act if we are to achieve peace. Hobbes's first law of nature is "that every man divest himself of the right he hath to all things by nature." The reason, again, is peace: "For when divers men have right not only to all things else, but to another's persons, if they use the same, there ariseth thereby invasion on the one part, and resistance on the other, which is war; and therefore contrary to the law of nature, the sum whereof consisteth in making peace" (I, 15, 2). In this way, Hobbes is able to reintroduce into his laws of nature the traditional hierarchical opposition of virtues and vices: charity and cruelty, justice and injustice, equity and arrogance, gratitude and ingratitude.

Hobbes's systematic analysis of natural law thus establishes a coherent theory of obligation. But what is its relation to his earlier analysis of human nature? It has recently been asserted that "Hobbes's ethical doctrine proper" can be "disengaged from an egoistic psychology, with which it has no logically necessary connection"[8] and that "a denial of Hobbes's psychology" can leave "his theory of obligation, in the proper sense unaffected."[9] But if it is difficult to demonstrate a logical connection between Hobbes's account of the laws of nature and his psychology, it is easy to show that his intention is to formulate a theory that will conform to "experience." Hobbes distinguishes, for example, between a "free gift" made "without consideration of reciprocal benefit, past, present, or to come" and a contract based upon "mutual donation" (I, 15, 7). In Hobbes's view, a free gift "carrieth with it no obligation greater than that which is enforced by the words. For he that promiseth to give, without any other consideration but his own affection, so long as he hath not given, deliberateth still, according as the causes of his affections continue or diminish; and he that deliberateth hath not yet willed, because the will is the last act of his deliberation" (I, 15, 7).

Even in contracts, Hobbes distinguishes sharply between those performed in the present and those to be performed in the future. The latter are based upon trust, which Hobbes defines as a covenant or promise to perform the terms of a contract. In contracts based upon trust, Hobbes warns that "he that performeth first, considering the disposition of men to take advantage of every thing for their benefit, doth but betray himself thereby to the covetousness, or other passion of him with whom he contracteth" (I, 15, 10). It follows that such covenants are not valid, until a power has been established which will compel men to obey their contracts.

In this pessimistic frame of mind, Hobbes revised themes that had been treated differently by philosophers of natural law before him. For instance, he opposed the traditional notion that promises "extorted from men by fear" are not binding. To Hobbes, there is "no reason why that which we do upon fear, should be less firm than that which we do for covetousness." Hobbes asks, with his characteristic blunt common sense, "What prisoner in war might be trusted to seek his ransom, and ought not rather to be killed, if he were not tied by the grant of his life, to perform his promise[?]" (I, 15, 13). A similar revision for a similar reason can be seen in Hobbes's treatment of political relations. Aristotle had argued that some men by nature "are worthy to govern, and others to serve." Although Hobbes's polemic against Aristotle rests upon the law that "*every man acknowledge other for his equal*" (I, 17, 1), it never actually denies Aristotle's view that men are inherently unequal. Rather it arises from Hobbes's "low" view of human nature. What prevents men from agreeing among themselves on who should govern whom is their propensity to vanity and self-deception. To Hobbes, it is perfectly self-evident that "every one naturally think[s] himself as able, at the least, to govern one another, as another to govern him" (I, 171). Since such a condition engenders conflict, it is incumbent upon men, even though they may think themselves superior, to acknowledge others as their equals.

This section shares the same pessimistic attitude that informs the earlier chapters on human nature. Hobbes attempts to inject a dose of realism into what he saw as the inflated rhetoric of natural law in the same way that he earlier tried to ground his theorems of human nature on something more solid than "castles in the air." Although the assumption of Hobbes's argument is not that all men are evil or wicked, he warns that if the laws of nature should be observed by some, and not by others, it would leave the good without defence against the wicked (I, 17, 10). As a consequence, he posits as another law of nature that those particular laws be so far observed as they subject us not to any danger (I, 17, 10). From this it follows that until a coercive power has been established which will compel men to obey the laws of nature, it suffices for men simply to desire their obedience; "the law of nature is not *in foro externo* [in act] till there be security for men to obey it; but is always *in foro interno* [in conscience], wherein the action of obedience being unsafe, the will and readiness to perform is taken for the performance" (I, 17, 10).

By concentrating upon the discrepancy between an internal and an external obligation to obey the laws of nature, Hobbes makes the relation of this obligation to his pessimistic view of human nature clear. The universality, the magisterial quality, the note of impartial judgment — all demand that human nature be put into a proper and balanced perspective. Whatever revisions Hobbes may have made in traditional natural law theory, his stress upon the difference between theory and practice suits his intention of reducing the passions, so prominent in his earlier discussion, to their proper significance. In this way, the individual becomes a member of a larger body whose propensities can be judged against a universal standard.

How precise are the judgments which Hobbes makes has not always been acknowledged. The laws of nature are plainly noble and lofty principles, but Hobbes is not afraid to allow us a glimpse of the petty passions beneath them: "it must necessarily be implied as a law of nature, *That no man reproach, revile, or deride or any otherwise, declare his hatred, contempt, or disesteem of any other.* But this law is very little practised. For what is more ordinary than reproaches of those that are rich, towards them that are not? or of those that sit in place of judicature, towards those that are accused at the bar? although to grieve them in that manner, be no part of the punishment for their crime, nor contained in their office" (I, 16, 11). This momentary glimpse of human perversity and senseless cruelty suggests the inadequacy of the view that the laws of nature are confined in Hobbes's theory to a narrowly conceived self-interest. Hobbes's point here is that those who violate the law that no man reproach another are so secure that they have no reason to fear reprisal. Nor can this comment be interpreted as a cynical observation aimed at undercutting the principle that prefaces it. Indeed Hobbes's perspective is so clearly and consistently defined, his point of view so plain, that he can afford to elaborate upon the reality that has so often prevented the laws of nature from being practiced without for a moment losing sight of their ultimate validity.

In spite of the majesty of Hobbes's laws of nature, they are ultimately impotent in the face of the persistence of human passions to achieve peace as a condition of security. Hobbes's own solution to the persistence of human unreason is the need for a common power to overawe us all. Hobbes chooses to withhold this solution until chapter nineteen, the last chapter of part one, to make its urgency appear more starkly clear and more compelling. In Hobbes's view, the laws of nature, though dictates of reason, are contrary to man's natural passions. Even "that consent (by which I understand the concurrence of many men's wills to one action) is not sufficient security for their common peace, without the erection of some common power, by the fear whereof they may be compelled both to keep the peace amongst themselves, and to join their strengths together against a common enemy" (I, 19, 6).

By thus emphasizing that for the effective enforcement of covenants, there should be a common power backed by force and able to punish, Hobbes means to affirm, as Leslie Stephen observed, that "political society is not essential to man as man. It is a product of his voluntary action and therefore implies conscious deliberation."[10] Such a deliberation necessarily involves a choice. Political society can provide a physical security unknown in man's natural state, but this security is not obtained without a price. The price is the permanent loss of natural liberty: "when a man covenanteth to subject his will to the command of another, he obligeth himself to this, that he resign his strength and means to him, whom he covenanteth to obey; and hereby, he that is to command may by the use of all their means and strength, be able by the terror thereof, to frame the will of them all to unity and concord among themselves" (I, 19, 7). The only way therefore that peace can be secured is for every man "to lay by or relinquish his own right of resisting him to whom he so transferreth it " (I, 19, 10). There is no other means, Hobbes believes, by which civil society can come into being, and from this belief he will proceed in part two to deduce his theory of sovereignty.

## II   De Corpore Politico

The attempt to formulate universally valid truths, discoverable by reason and deduction, led Hobbes to minimize all concrete, historical manifestations of power in his search for the primary forms of government. But it was only in the theory of sovereignty — the most abstract part of Hobbes's political thought — that this tendency reached its logical conclusion in a thoroughgoing rationalism of the most uncompromising sort. Hobbes's conception of unitary sovereignty was consciously inspired by the abstract purity of geometric theorems. It was felt by Hobbes to share the same rigor as his formulation of natural law. Moreover, of the three ways in which the body politic originates — by covenant, by conquest, and by birth — government by covenant was seen by Hobbes as the product of the unanimous consent of a people living in a natural state. It was thus the most basic form of government.

### 1.   *The Generation of Government*

In his initial discussion of sovereignty which takes up the first chapter of part two, Hobbes is concerned with certain general principles relating to everything he will subsequently say. The topic with which Hobbes begins is a fundamental one — the question of "how a multitude of persons natural are united by covenants into one person civil, or body politic" (II, 1, 1). Though this topic was traditional in political thought, Hobbes was clearly combating several prevailing contemporary attitudes. He opposed a modern version of the classical theory of mixed sovereignty which supposed the power of making laws given to a democratic assembly, the power of judging laws given to another assembly; and the power of administering the laws given to yet a third assembly, or to some individual (II, 1, 15). He also disagreed with the attitude that forces raised to defend the commonwealth against an outside enemy should be limited by the subjects (II, 1, 14). Furthermore, he did not believe that the commonwealth is a government of laws not men (II, 1, 13).

In opposition to these attitudes, Hobbes insists that sovereignty cannot be conferred conditionally. The generation of the commonwealth, in his view, is a covenant made by the unanimous concurrence of all men who upon the establishment of the commonwealth become subjects to the sovereign. This point is important. Hobbes's argument that consent must be unanimous enables him to emphasize more easily the indivisible nature of sovereign power. Only by the unanimous consent of all to unite the sovereign power in one body — whether an individual or an assembly — can the danger of a return to the natural state of war be avoided. If this principle is valid, it follows that an assembly, such as a parliament, can have no rights independent of the monarch, when the monarch is the sovereign. The monarch may make use of a parliament or of other administrative branches in governing the commonwealth. But these bodies do not enjoy part of the sovereignty nor are they coequal with the monarch in the exercise of powers. Among his prerogatives, the sovereign has the power to raise unlimited forces against an enemy "which we cannot limit" (II, 1, 14). A more important prerogative is that of judging what doctrines are to be taught. In man's natural state, the individual is judge of good and evil and must follow his conscience because he has no other guide to follow. But, in the commonwealth, he relinquishes his conscience along with his natural liberty. The sovereign makes the "politic or civil" laws, which are the public conscience, the determination of "what is good, and what is bad, and what he ought to do, and what not" (II, 1, 10).

Such an argument, combined with the austerity and conceptual rigor of its more extreme results in *The Elements of Law,* might seem prophetic of modern totalitarianism. Significantly enough, it was not until the twentieth century that Hobbes's political theory was first subjected to systematic scrutiny.[11] Yet to construe

Hobbes's political thought exclusively in twentieth century terms is to misunderstand it.

What separates Hobbes from modern apologists of totalitarianism is his awareness of the instability of power. "What emerges from his doctrine," writes Howard Warrender, "is the inherent weakness of the sovereign."[12] As much as he wished for the advance of physical security, Hobbes did not wholly subscribe to the belief that the sovereign is all-powerful. Indeed, the arguments that appear in *The Elements of Law* are, if anything, a rebuttal to the notion that the sovereign is capable in Warrender's words "of governing through the terror of his sanctions alone."[13] The actual manifestation of political power is susceptible to erosion from without and within. From without, it is susceptible to invasion by a superior power; if this should occur, "then is every man, by necessity of nature, allowed to make the best provision he can for himself; and thus is the private sword, and the estate of war again reduced" (II, 1, 14). From within, it is susceptible to subversion. Should anyone doubt that political power is not self-sufficient, Hobbes uses the most emphatic terms to describe the consequences of rebellion. Without the unanimous consent of all citizens, "the power of the body politic (the essence whereof is the non-resistance of the members) is none, nor the body politic of any benefit" (II, 1, 18). In contrast to the formulations of modern ideologues, such a reservation seems negative, if not downright pessimistic. What it demands is not total sacrifice to a higher truth but an exchange in which one good — natural liberty — is given up for a better one — physical security.

## 2. *The Forms of Government*

Conventional treatises on politics usually began with a discussion of the various forms of government. In chapter two and chapter five of part two, Hobbes followed this procedure; like many writers on politics in the seventeenth century, he expressed a clear preference for monarchy over democracy and aristocracy. But in *The Elements of Law,* this discussion is subordinated to Hobbes's theory of unitary sovereignty. As a result, it fails to achieve the same degree of certainty and conviction as more traditional arguments. As Hobbes himself confessed in the preface to *De Cive,* his preference for monarchy was the one element in his political thought "not to be demonstrated but only probably stated" (EW, II, xxii).

Just as Hobbes's opposition to the classical theory of mixed sovereignty served to distinguish his position from the theories of seventeenth century republicans, so his failure to demonstrate the view that monarchy is the best form of government serves to distinguish his political thought from that of seventeenth century apologists for the divine right of kings. Indeed his outlook appears to have less in common with the theory of the divine right of kings than we might suppose. Set alongside Hobbes's fear of the reversion of society to a state of war, the triumphalist politics of divine right theorists radiates assurance, not alarm. While divine right theorists affirmed the sacred, providential character of monarchy, they did not perceive a conflict between divine sanction and human needs. Hobbes does not address himself to such a conflict, but he does demand that government continually justify itself by the fairly rigorous standard of personal security. Finally the thrust of divine right theorists was towards an apotheosis of the person of the king — an apotheosis expressed by analogies to such scriptural types as Moses, David, and even Christ. By contrast, Hobbes insists more aggressively than they would dare on the humanity and weakness of the monarch. Any "inconvenience" in conferring power on one man stems "not from the power, but from the affections and passions which reign in every one, as well monarch as subject" (II, 5, 4).

Despite Hobbes's failure to celebrate the glories of monarchy, his taste was monarchic — and remained so. He disdained democracy as the "government of a few orators" and was convinced that "the passions of many men" are more violent, when, as in an aristocracy, they are assembled together, than "the passions of one man alone" (II, 5, 4). But Hobbes's point of view is wholly different from that of divine right theorists. In contrast to their triumphant celebration of the virtues of the god-like king, Hobbes regarded power as something potentially liable to abuse. Hence his preference for monarchy rests upon the belief that of the three forms of government monarchy is the one under which threats to security and "outrages upon the people" are likely to be minimized (II, 5, 6). As Hobbes's contemporary critics were well aware, such a limited claim for kingship could never become the basis for the glorification of any of the existing ruling houses of Europe.

From the divine right theorists, Hobbes retains the absolutist imperative to preserve the succession of the existing government.

But, unlike patriarchalists like Robert Filmer, Hobbes resolutely refuses to identify the present government with the origin of government — whether democratic or despotic — or to provide present rulers with such spiritual ancestors as Adam, Arthur, or Brutus. In fact, the recurring possibility of different combinations or permutations of government is one of the minor themes of Hobbes's discussion of the forms of government in *The Elements of Law*. As an origin of government, democracy is an extremely volatile form. In itself only an aristocracy in disguise, democracy turns into an aristocracy or monarchy whenever "the particular members of the commonwealth" grow "weary of attendance at public courts, as dwelling far off" or become "attentive to their private businesses, and withal displeased with the government of the people" (II, 2, 6). In pre-Augustan Rome, the form of government was democracy, yet the capacity of the sovereign power to decentralize its administrative tasks assumed a bewildering complexity of forms: "at the same time they may have a council aristocratical, such as was the senate; and at the same time they may have a subordinate monarch, such as was their dictator, who had for a time the exercise of the whole sovereignty, and such as are all generals in war" (II, 1, 17). In elective or limited monarchies, where restraints are placed upon the exercise of power, the apparent sovereign reveals himself in fact to be the subject (II, 2, 10). Such permutations indicate that political forms are perceived in *The Elements of Law* to possess a greater volatility than in divine right theories.

### 3. *Obedience and Rebellion*

A principle concern of seventeenth century political writing and a prominent issue in Hobbes's political thought was the problem of legitimacy. A great deal of discussion centered on two related questions of how existing governments actually came into being and on what grounds they could compel allegiance. Hobbes addresses the first of these two questions in *The Elements of Law* by initially distinguishing between commonwealth "by institution" and commonwealth "by acquisition." A commonwealth by institution is established in the manner described in the first chapter, namely by a covenant of every man with every man. A commonwealth by acquisition, which Hobbes treats in the third chapter, occurs when sovereignty has been acquired by force. Hobbes goes on in the fourth chapter to introduce a third and distinct means by which governments claim allegiance — commonwealth by birth.

Hobbes's systematic enumeration of the ways "by which a man becometh subject to another" (II, 4, 1) clarifies the second question, how governments compel allegiance; but it also obscures the first question, how governments actually come into existence. It is evident that a government by acquisition or by birth possesses a more concrete relation to historical fact than government by institution. But while it is improbable that Hobbes believed that any existing governments actually originated through an explicit covenant, he granted the same status to all three kinds. All three are equally legitimate; in all three the sovereign possesses the same rights.

Despite this equality, Hobbes suggests that commonwealth by acquisition and by birth do in actuality have a more insecure foundation than commonwealth by institution. This conclusion can be inferred from the fact that Hobbes resorts to analogy rather than deduction to account for the existence of these two less stable commonwealths. For commonwealth by acquisition, Hobbes took as his model the master-servant relationship; for commonwealth by birth, the parent-child relationship. Perhaps as a consequence of proving by analogy, certain aspects of Hobbes's analysis are perplexing. He makes clear that the master-servant relationship is valid only so long as the master entrusts the servant with freedom of mobility. According to Hobbes, "that servant that is no longer trusted, but committed to his chains and custody, is thereby discharged of the obligation *in foro interno,* and therefore if he can get loose, may lawfully go his way" (II, 3, 7). Parents, however, are not subject to a similar restriction: "they may alienate them (their children), that is assign his or her dominion, by selling or giving them in adoption or servitude to others; or may pawn them for hostages, kill them for rebellion, or sacrifice them for peace" (II, 4, 8). It is not clear from this passage what could free the children from the obligation of obeying their parents. In any event, the notion of non-resistance implicit in the parent-child model is clearly incompatible with the inalienable right of self-preservation enunciated earlier.

Fortunately, however, Hobbes simply ignored the import of his own formulation and preserved the right of self-preservation by establishing an interrelationship between child and servant. A family consists of both children and servants. The model which

Hobbes invokes to represent the liberty of the subject is the Roman freeman — the child or servant who in Roman society is granted an "equality of favour" and "employments of honour," though not exempted in any way, from subjection and obedience to the sovereign (II, 4, 9).

In chapters six and seven, Hobbes goes on to examine the relation of church and state. Not surprisingly he defends a thoroughgoing Erastianism in which church is completely subordinated to state. In keeping with his theory of unitary sovereignty, Hobbes rejects any claim by clerics to possess a spiritual authority that is independent of the sovereign. He does not, however, deny the validity of Christian revelation. As a result, he bases his arguments, not upon logical deductions, as in earlier chapters, but upon the citation of passages from scripture — a reversion to a method of relying upon authority that Hobbes had earlier repudiated. But the conclusion is the same: "in no case can the sovereign power of a commonwealth be subject to any authority ecclesiastical, besides that of Christ himself" (II, 7, 10).

The eighth chapter, on the causes of rebellion, follows a basic strategy of limiting the grounds of disobedience as much as possible. Hobbes cites three factors that "dispose men to sedition": discontent, pretense of right, and hope of success. It is in Hobbes's treatment of the second factor — "pretence of right" — that we can see most clearly how *The Elements of Law* has been shaped by a desire to purge political theory of any grounds for disobedience, save physical self-preservation. By making the sovereign include the judicial, the deliberative, and the executive branch, Hobbes was able to oppose the view that laws and property possess an autonomous status in the commonwealth (II, 8, 8). By insisting that the word "body politic" signified "not the concord, but the union of many men" (II, 8, 7), Hobbes was able to oppose the view that the subject possesses a power independent of and over against the sovereign. Hence tyrannicide becomes logically impossible since there can exist no "power of judicature" exclusive of the sovereign, which could decide such a case (II, 8, 10). In these uncompromising formulations, a new response to classical political theory can be sensed, as if Hobbes had resolved, once and for all time, to eradicate the imaginary privileges and fanciful divisions introduced by proponents of a mixed or limited sovereignty.

Opposition to rebellion did not, however, imply — as it does in the twentieth century — total conformity to a prevailing political ideology. For it is assumed in *The Elements of Law* that the duty of non-resistance formed a solid foundation for civil government, above which the individual conscience might freely soar, but beneath which sedition could only undermine. Hence it is possible for Hobbes to declare: "no human law is intended to oblige the conscience of a man, but the actions only" (II, 6, 3). In the highly civilized atmosphere of the Hobbesian body politic, the indulgence of private speculation is freely permitted, but its public display is strictly prohibited.

Thus the importance of the private conscience, which is central to our conception of liberty, was an anathema to Hobbes. Nothing brings this out more clearly than his discussion of law in the tenth and final chapter of part two. In Hobbes's view civil law is the only standard by which the actions of subjects are to be judged, "to determine, whether they be right or wrong, profitable or unprofitable, virtuous or vicious" (II, 10, 8). The rigor of Hobbes's formulation has always proved difficult to comprehend. For Hobbes does not deny that such terms as "right and wrong, profitable and unprofitable, etc." are objective concepts, transcendental norms, or divine laws. He simply insists that in society men cannot agree on what they are. As a result, men's beliefs about what is right and wrong are reduced to the status of subjective opinions, which each person invokes for his own private interest. Implicit in such an argument is that there must be general agreement in ethical matters. By insisting on such an agreement, Hobbes rules out controversy. For Hobbes, the only norms which can satisfy this criteria are civil laws, laws which emanate from the sovereign and hence from the body politic in general.

But why does Hobbes base the norms of civil law upon will — the consent of nations — when he had earlier based the norms of natural law upon reason — logical argument? The answer appears to lie in his theory of social contract. When man enters into civil society, he gives up the right to exercise his reason in matters of right and wrong, choosing instead to accept the civil law which must conform to natural law insofar as it leads to peace but which by the tacit consent of the sovereign may also include custom and opinion (II, 10, 10). This distinction may help to explain why Hobbes's discussion of man's natural state and of natural laws appears to be demonstrated and his discussion of matters concerning civil society only probably stated.

The essential elements of Hobbes's political theory are completely assembled in *The Elements of Law.* In *De Cive* and *Leviathan,* he added refinements, clarified obscure phraseology, and strengthened certain aspects of his argument, but the interlocking chain of deductions set forth in his first treatise remained basically intact. It was in matters which Hobbes regarded not as logically demonstrated but as only probably stated that he made major changes in the later works. In general the chapters dealing with what he viewed as probably stated are not only far less original and less compelling but also more susceptible to revision in subsequent works.

*The Elements of Law* thus represents an advanced stage of Hobbes's thought. It does not show how certain conclusions were reached; instead it attempts to prove that such conclusions are valid. Since these conclusions, which are illustrated and confirmed by "experience" — the non-scientific equivalent of experiment — can become the starting point for arguments through which their implications are applied to specific situations, there is no reason why Hobbes had to confine himself to the Euclidean model in presenting his argument. Indeed it may have been his awareness of the austerity and lack of popular appeal of the geometric model formulated in all of its rigor in *The Elements of Law* that led him to modify it in *De Cive* in favor of a more persuasive mode of expression.

CHAPTER 4

# De Cive

*D*e *Cive,* like *The Elements of Law,* was originally cast in the
form of a scientific treatise; it followed the pattern for theoretical investigation which had been set by such works as Galileo's
*De Motu* (1590) or Harvey's *De Motu Cordis* (1628). Hobbes's
intention in *De Cive* was to do for politics what others had been
doing for astronomy, physics, and anatomy: to discover the underlying laws of motion. Printed "privately" in Paris in 1642, in a
small edition bearing only the initials T.H. on the title page, it was
addressed chiefly to a select group of scientists and dilletanti. When
a larger edition was published by Samuel Sorbiére in Amsterdam in
1647, some important notes, a dedication, and a famous "Preface
to the Reader" were added. By the time Hobbes came to publish an
English translation of *De Cive* in 1651, he had departed from the
original pattern: *Philosophical Rudiments concerning Government
and Society* adheres to the form of an elementary textbook for
beginners. Hobbes changed genres for the same reason that he
composed *De Cive* before the first two parts of the system of which
it was to form the conclusion: he was engrossed in the political con-
flicts which were going on in England at the same time. As he
declared in the preface, "Whilst I contrive, order, pensively and
slowly compose these matters; (for I only do reason, I dispute not);
it so happened in the interim, that my country some few years
before the civil wars did rage, was boiling hot with questions
concerning the rights of dominion . . . and was the cause which, all
those other matters deferred, ripened and plucked from me this
third part" (EW, II, xx). Thus, while Hobbes was writing about
politics in the general terms of a natural philosopher, he was also
taking up issues of political immediacy as a humanist.

74

The method of argument which Hobbes used in *De Cive* was adapted to his practical aims. Logic and experience were the two sources from which he had drawn material in *The Elements of Law* to demonstrate his theory. Though Hobbes continued to strengthen the logical sequence of propositions developed in *The Elements of Law,* he turned increasingly to experience in *De Cive* as an empirical witness to the validity of these propositions. "Grounded on its own principles sufficiently known by experience," *De Cive,* he believed, "would not stand in need of the former sections" (EW, II, xx). Hobbes was eager to state as forcefully as he could the principles he thought necessary to impress upon his readers, but he did not believe his system was one in which every axiom must be apprehended in the proper order.

In seeking ways to present his theory more effectively, Hobbes maintained the same organization of chapters developed in the last section of *Human Nature* and in *De Corpore Politico* but clarified the arrangement of those chapters. He divided *De Cive* into three parts, each with a different theme. The first part, "Liberty," deals with the state of nature and with the laws of nature; the second, "Dominion," is occupied with what Hobbes regards as the major political issues of the time: the origin of civil society; the various forms of government; the causes of the dissolution of the commonwealth; and the duties of the sovereign. The third part, "Religion," is concerned with the relationship of church and state. The section on religion, the only one of the three topics to undergo major expansion from *The Elements of Law,* reflects Hobbes's belief that a connection existed between the diminution of civil sovereignty in England and the power which the clergy enjoyed.

## I  *"The Author's Preface to the Reader"*

Because Hobbes approaches political theory in *De Cive* with the interest and educative aims of a humanist, his treatment of human nature undergoes a slight change of emphasis. In *De Cive* Hobbes retains the main ideas of *The Elements of Law* but puts them into a significantly different setting. In Hobbes's analysis of the passions in part one, chapter nine of *The Elements of Law,* it was clear that he believed that feelings of superiority and glory, and the drive for power, were as "natural" as the desire for self-preservation. In the preface to *De Cive,* he vehemently denies that such an argument

leads to the doctrine that men are "wicked by nature." Rather by
nature they are like children who "unless you give (them) all they
ask for ... are peevish and cry, aye, and strike their parents sometimes; and all this they have done from nature" (EW, II, xvi). Significantly, Hobbes omits from *De Cive* the chapters dealing with
human nature in *The Elements of Law.* Indeed he suggests that the
state of childhood is only temporary, for men come to "be better
governed through good education and experience" (EW, II, xvii).
Hobbes sums up his position by declaring "unless therefore we will
say that men are naturally evil, because they receive not their
education and use of reason from nature, we must needs acknowledge that men may derive desire, fear, anger, and other passions
from nature, and yet not impute the evil effects of those unto
nature" (EV, II, vii). Echoes of this view are equally prominent in
the main body of *De Cive.* When Hobbes comes to oppose the
Aristotelian theory that "man is a creature born fit for society," he
affirms the humanist ideal that "man is made fit for society not by
nature but by education" (EW, II, 2).

This belief in the importance of education in fitting man to live in
society leads Hobbes to demand the suppression of what he regards
as "false doctrines" concerning "civil knowledge." A series of
rhetorical flourishes give emphasis to his insistence in the preface
that much of the present turbulence had arisen from the promulga-
tion of such false doctrines:

How many kings, and those good men too, hath this one error, that a
tyrant kind might lawfully be put to death, been the slaughter of! How
many throats hath this false position cut, that a prince for some causes
may by some certain men be deposed! And what bloodshed hath not this
erroneous doctrine caused, that kings are not superiors to, but adminis-
trators for the multitude! Lastly, how many rebellions hath this opinion
been the cause of, which teacheth that the knowledge whether the commands of kings be just or unjust, belongs to private men; and that before
they yield obedience, they not only may, but ought to dispute them! (EW,
II, xi–xii)

Since the propagation of these false doctrines naturally endangers
the effectiveness of the sovereign, the program for education out-
lined by Hobbes in the preface requires for its implementation the
refutation if not the elimination of false hypotheses. Hobbes's

principles in *De Cive* are a means to carry out this operation insofar as possible. Paradoxically, Hobbes formulates principles that today might be called "realistic" for a reason that now seems very "unrealistic" — namely, to bring about a radical change in outlook on the part of his countrymen.

Yet, it is evident that Hobbes had no illusions about the realization of his educational aims. In *De Cive* he finally acknowledges that it is practically impossible to construct a theory that would be immune from criticism and makes it clear that he is willing to settle for something less. Rather than erect a system that is above dispute, he now seeks to minimize the controversial aspects of his theory. His aim, writes Hobbes, is "to offend none besides those whose principles these contradict, and whose tender minds are lightly offended by every difference of opinions" (EW, II, xxiii). To achieve this aim, Hobbes's main technique is to do all that is humanly possible to avoid particular cases and to confine himself to the general features of his doctrine (EW, II, xxii–xxiii).

By refusing to make more than modest claims for his theory, Hobbes obviously hopes to avoid arousing the passions of others. If the reader understands his doctrine correctly, he will prefer to endure "with patience some inconveniences under government, (because human affairs cannot possibly be without some), than self-opinionatedly disturb the quiet of the public" (EW, II, xxi). Hobbes ridicules as naïve the belief of his readers that war brings change: "you will esteem it better to enjoy yourselves in the present state, though perhaps not the best, than by waging war endeavour to procure a reformation for other men in another age" (EW, II, xxi). Such an argument does not ask us to subordinate our passions to the hypothetical structure of a truly unified society. It tells us to accept an existing society that is something more than barbarous but less than ideal.

## 1. *"Of Liberty"*

Part one of *De Cive* comprises four chapters, dealing first with the state of men outside civil society, then with the laws of nature, and finally with the identity of natural and divine law. These chapters correspond to the section of *The Elements of Law* which extends from chapter fourteen in part one through the end of chapter eighteen. Hobbes follows the order of the earlier work in *De Cive* exactly, except when he combines chapters sixteen and seventeen of *The Elements of Law* to form chapter three. Many of the stylistic changes which take place between *The Elements of Law* and the English translation of *De Cive* can be explained by Hobbes's desire to reach a larger audience. Latin terms like *de foro interno* and *de foro externo* are replaced by literal English equivalents. Hobbes seems more willing to relax the severity of logical deduction to accommodate the more comprehensible mode of analogy. An elaborate comparison of "the diversity of dispositions" in men entering society with the diversity of stones brought together in a building (EW, II, 36) characterizes the new approach. Even more important, terms are defined more precisely. Reason becomes right reason; man's natural state becomes the state of nature. The state of war which had been broadly defined in *The Elements of Law* as "the will and intention of contending by force is either by words or actions sufficiently declared" (I, 14, 11), is now defined "as a mere war, and not that simply, but a war of all men against all men" (EW, II, 11). What had originally been a generalized notion of mutual distrust is transformed into a powerful symbol of anarchy and disorder.

Chapter one, of "Liberty," establishes the grounds for believing that the state of nature is a state of war. Since Hobbes has omitted the analysis of man and his passions that provided the framework for this proposition in *The Elements of Law,* he bases his contention on the self-contained argument that "man is not born fit for society." Hobbes's main task in chapter one is how to prove this argument. In the absence of a supporting chain of deductions, he tries to demonstrate it through an appeal to experience. In a long footnote, in which Hobbes takes cognizance of criticisms of his position, he denies that it entails the view that men are naturally unsociable. It is not man's natural benevolence but his natural weakness which makes him sociable. Regardless of age, writes Hobbes, men "have need of others to help them live" (EW, II, 2). Hobbes assumes that this natural human insufficiency is so obvious as to require no further elaboration. He denies, however, that a natural need for others is accompanied by a natural love for others: "for if by nature one man should love another, that is, as man, there could be no reason returned why every man should not equally love every man, as being equally man; or why he should rather frequent those, whose society affords him honour or profit"

(EW, II, 3). This thesis is then sustained in the main body of the chapter by observation of why "men do meet":

For if they meet for traffic, it is plain every man regards not his fellow, but his business; if to discharge some office, a certain market-friendship is begotten, which hath more of jealousy in it than true love, and whence factions sometimes may arise, but good will never; if for pleasure and recreation of mind, every man is wont to please himself most with those things which stir up laughter, whence he may, according to the nature of that which is riduculous, by comparison of another man's defects and infirmities, pass the more current in his own opinion. And although this be sometimes innocent and without offence, yet it is manifest they are not so much delighted with the society, as their own vain glory. But for the most part, in these kinds of meeting we wound the absent; their whole life, sayings, actions are examined, judged, condemned. (EW, II, 3-4)

Hobbes's attempt to appeal to experience in refuting the view that man is born fit for society contributes to another novelty in *De Cive:* the exclusive emphasis upon vainglory. In *The Elements of Law,* Hobbes had granted a legitimate (though limited) status to glory, based upon "a just valuation" of the self in relation to others. Now the only person whom Hobbes singles out for praise is the "temperate man" who "permits as much to others as he assumes to himself" (EW, II, 7). By contrast, the discord that arises from the contentions of vainglorious men are "the fiercest." It follows that there are "no wars so sharply waged as between sects of the same religion, and factions of the same commonwealth, where the contestation is either concerning doctrines or politic prudence" (EW, II, 7-8).

Hobbes evidently came to recognize the vulnerability of an argument which seeks to determine the behavior of men in the state of nature by observing their actions in society, for he did not return to it in *Leviathan.* Rousseau objected to Hobbes's argument and charged that Hobbes was one of those who "has transferred to the state of nature ideas which were acquired in society; so that, in speaking of the savage, they described the social man."[1] As Rousseau implies, an argument of nature cannot be confirmed by appealing to society. Rousseau believed that the cause of conflict is an exploitative, competitive society which gives every incentive for anarchy.[2] This society has failed to achieve a viable means of uniting warring individuals. In short, Hobbes was not sufficiently precise in Rousseau's opinion, because he did not distinguish sharply enough between natural man and social man.

Hobbes reveals in a later chapter, however, that he perceives at least one difference between natural man and social man. In the state of nature, man fears violent death by bodily assault; in civil society, this fear is displaced by the fear of punishment. Nonetheless, another fear makes its appearance, fear of shame and humiliation by slander and derision: "... because all signs of hatred and contempt provoke most of all to brawling and fighting, insomuch as most men would rather lose their lives (that I say, not their peace) than suffer slander; it follows in the seventh place, that it is prescribed by the law of nature, that no man . . . *declare himself to hate or scorn another"* (EW, II, 38). In civil society, verbal aggression occupies an analogous position to physical aggression in the state of nature. It is an error, however, to think that Hobbes subscribed to the behavior he observed. Both kinds of conduct, however universal, were to Hobbes's way of thinking deplorable, because both were inimical to the peace which all men should rationally desire. Like John Bunyan, Hobbes viewed society for the most part as a vanity fair. And like Bunyan, he does not seem to have enjoyed or approved of the spectacle.

In the next three chapters, Hobbes takes up the laws of nature. This subject is one of the most controversial in Hobbes's political thought. In conflicting accounts, we are told by commentators that the laws of nature are either rational theorems of prudence[3] or universal laws with transcendent foundations, which we ought to obey simply because they command us to.[4] Since these conflicting interpretations have given rise to the charge that Hobbes was inconsistent, it may be useful to examine them in the context of Hobbes's discussion of natural law in *De Cive*.

In chapter two, Hobbes defines a law of nature as a "dictate of right reason, conversant about those things which are either to be done or omitted for the constant preservation of life and members, as much as in us lies" (EW, II, 16). This definition is an expansion of Hobbes's brief statement in *The Elements of Law* that the laws of nature "declare unto us the ways of peace" (I, 15, 1). It is based on the assumption, which Hobbes clearly regards as self-evident, that "every man is desirous of what is good for him, and shuns what is evil, but chiefly the chiefest of natural evils, which is death; and this he doth by a certain impulsion of nature, no less than that whereby a stone moves downward'' (EW, II, 8).[5] So stated, this assumption becomes a natural right to self-preservation. Since the individual is the only judge of this right to self-preservation, a law of nature is evidently a dictate of rational prudence, a form of natural rather than moral obligation. If no man is obliged to relinquish his natural right to self-preservation, it is no longer possible to insist that the laws of nature are always binding duties: ''the law of nature doth always and everywhere oblige us in the internal court, or that of conscience; but not always in the external court, but then only when it may be done with safety'' (EW, II, 46). Significantly, Hobbes's contemporary adversaries found both aspects of this doctrine disturbing: to them it represented a watering down of traditional natural law theory which held that the laws of nature are transcendent and should always be obeyed.

On the other hand, a passage in chapter three has been used to justify the argument that Hobbes's laws of nature have a universality that distinguishes them from expediency.[6] Explaining the difference between a just act and the justice of a person, Hobbes declares:

These words, *just* and *unjust,* as also *justice* and *injustice,* are equivocal; for they signify one thing when they are attributed to persons, another when to actions. When they are attributed to actions, *just* signifies as much as what is done with right, and *unjust,* as what is done with injury. He who hath done some just thing, is not therefore said to be a *just* person, but *guiltless;* and he that hath done some unjust thing, we do not therefore say he is an *unjust,* but *guilty* man. But when the words are applied to persons, *to be just* signifies as much to be delighted in just dealing, to study how to do righteousness, or to endeavour in all things to do that which is just; and *to be unjust* is to neglect rightoues dealing, or to think it is to be measured not according to my contract, but some present benefit. So as the justice or injustice of the mind, the intention, or the man, is one thing, that of an action or omission another; and innumerable actions of a just man may be unjust, and of an unjust man, just. But that man is to be accounted just, who doth just things because the law commands it, unjust things only by reason of his infirmity; and he is properly said to be unjust, who doth righteousness for fear of the punishment annexed unto the law, and unrighteousness by reason of the iniquity of his mind. (EW, II, 32–33)

How can such diametrically opposed viewpoints be found in the same section of a single book?

In order to answer this question, it may be helpful to examine the above passage in the context of the argument in which it occurs. It is part of Hobbes's discussion of the second law of nature which obliges us "to *perform contracts* or *to keep trust*" (EW, II, 29), for "in vain would contracts be made, unless we stood to them" (EW, II, 30). The alternatives are "a declared war, or a sure and faithful peace" (EW, II, 30). For Hobbes this law is a source of justice and injustice. Where there is no covenant, there can be neither justice nor injustice; but when a covenant has been made, to break it is an unjust action. For Hobbes "an unjust action" becomes synonymous with "breach of contract and trust" (EW, II, 31).

A special case of the law of nature which obliges us to perform our contracts is our obligation to obey the sovereign's commands. Since a person who covenants with other persons to give up his right of governing himself to another also gives up his right as an individual to decide what is just and what is unjust, it is no longer possible for him to perform this obligation and also endeavor "in all things" to do that which is just. A sovereign may wage an unjust war, as Hobbes later says, but the subject discharges his conscience and obligation simply by keeping his contract to obey the sovereign's commands. Actions conforming to these commands may be unjust, but if they are, the sovereign will have to answer for them. This is a distinction few of us would care to accept unreservedly, but it illustrates how the main thrust of Hobbes's political philosophy directed him away from the formulation of an ethics such as we know it.

But if the subject's obligations in the state of nature are reduced to a single obligation in civil society, it applies in all cases. At times a person may be required to keep his covenant in defiance of some "present benefit." Even the person who keeps the covenant must first of all recognize his allegiance to it as his personal obligation. At this point in Hobbes's long chain of reasoning, applied to a specific command, is the central question to which the notion of the covenant directed all ethical endeavour — not to an obligation imposed by threat of external punishment, since power alone is insufficient to bind the individual, but to an obligation which is self-imposed. Even this obligation, however, appears to fit naturally into the broader setting of Hobbes's theory. A desire for "present benefit" is opposed to a desire for self-preservation, not to a disinterested good or duty. Indeed, it is hard to see how a conception of duty could have any place in Hobbes's thought. The attention of his natural philosophy was focused upon the causes of phenomena, and his principle ethical concepts were directed, not upon a moral principle which is independent of all natural desires, but upon the desires which move men to just or unjust actions. A desire for present benefits can be a cause of unjust actions. Some other, more fundamental desire, must oppose it.[7]

Hobbes's enumeration of the laws of nature differs slightly in each of his major works. In *De Cive,* Hobbes makes a distinction between "fundamental" and "special" laws of nature. Besides the "fundamental" law of nature that "peace be sought after," Hobbes cites in the second chapter of *De Cive* the first "special" law of nature "that the right of all men to all things ought not to be retained; but that some certain rights ought to be transferred or relinquished" (EW, II, 17). Although a man cannot be required to relinquish his right to defend himself, it is necessary for him to lay down his right to all things: "for if every one should retain his right to all things, it must necessarily follow that some by right might invade, and others, by the same right, might defend themselves against them.... Therefore, war would follow" (EW, II, 17).

As we have seen, the second law of nature is that men "perform their contracts." The third precept of the laws of nature is the law of ingratitude: "that you suffer not him to be the worse for you, who, out of the confidence he had in you, first did you a good turn; or that you accept not a gift, but with a mind to endeavour that the giver shall have no just occasion to repent him of his gift" (EW, II, 35). Without this law of nature, benevolence would be impossible, "neither would there be aught of mutual assistance among them, nor any commencement of gaining grace and favour" (EW, II, 35). But since this law does not involve a breach of trust or contract, for no contract has passed among the parties, a breach of it is not an act of injustice but an act of ingratitude.

In chapter three of *De Cive,* Hobbes goes on to list the twenty laws of nature. These laws and any others which may be discovered are binding because they appeal to the conscience. As soon as civil law and civil society come into being, however, logic shows that men must give up their right as individuals to decide between justice and injustice, meum and tuum, right and wrong. Once Hobbes had proceeded thus far, he encountered a question posed by his theory. If men are invariably in disagreement upon such basic issues, how can they agree upon anything? To answer this question, Hobbes added a section near the end of chapter three which deals with ethics in greater detail than in *The Elements of Law.* In the state of nature, men, because of their diverse constitutions, inclinations, and opinions, cannot agree on what is good and evil. Since this disagreement leads to a state of war, "as long as they are in it" men are able to agree on one thing: that the present state of war is evil and future peace is good.

In contrast to present good, however, future good does compel assent: "for things present are obvious to the sense, things to come to our reason only." Since reason declares that peace is good, all means to peace are good, including such virtues as "modesty, equity, trust, humanity, mercy" (EW, II, 48). Sense and reason are thus radically opposed. Reason requires the mastery of natural passions; nonetheless civil society cannot depend upon unaided human reason.[8] In *De Cive* Hobbes makes this point emphatically clear by insisting that "because men cannot put off this same irrational appetite, whereby they greedily prefer the present good ... before the future," in spite of their agreement concerning "the aforesaid virtues ... they disagree still concerning their nature, to wit, in what each of them doth consist." The perfect realization of ethical principles in society is simply impossible: "for as oft as another's good action displeaseth any man, that action hath the name given of some neighbouring vice; likewise the bad actions which please them, are ever intituled to some virtue. Whence it comes to pass that the same action is praised by these, and called virtue, and dispraised by those, and termed vice" (EW, II, 48). Hence the sovereign must perform as an arbiter of moral standards, albeit with the expectation that his own decisions will always fall short of justice in its ideal form.

## 2. *"Dominion"*

Hobbes's discussion of the body politic in "Dominion," part two of *De Cive,* is more extensive than the comparable section of *The Elements of Law;* seven out of the ten chapters are substantially expanded. These expansions are due in part to Hobbes's own elaboration of his ideas, and in part to his inclusion of more references relating to contemporary political issues. In enlarging these chapters, Hobbes shows again that his aim is educational: how to offer practical advice to his contemporaries, not how to construct an ideal state.

Perhaps the best way to perceive the educative aim of these chapters is to compare some passages of *De Cive* with parallel passages in *The Elements of Law.* Chapter five, "On the Causes and First Beginnings of Government," corresponds to the first chapter of *De Corpore Politico.* What Hobbes aims at in his expansions is greater clarification of his position. As we have seen, Hobbes's insistence that the body politic unite all warring individuals led him in *The Elements of Law* to insist that "every particular man" consent, not just "the greater number" (II, 1, 2). When revising this chapter in *De Cive,* Hobbes attempted to clarify this idea by inserting in parentheses that the consent of men "consists in this only . . . that they direct all their actions . . . to the common good" (EW, II, 65). In addition to including parentheses, Hobbes introduces a further explanation as to why consent must be supported by coercion: "somewhat else must be done, that those who have once consented for the common good to peace and mutual help, may by fear be restrained lest afterwards they again dissent, when their private interest shall appear discrepant from the common good" (EW, II, 66). Not all of the changes which Hobbes introduces in chapter five are for the purpose of clarification. In *The Elements of Law,* Hobbes sought to achieve a conceptual rigor that is possible only when words are used in their strict, literal signification. When composing *De Cive,* however, Hobbes seems to have relaxed this stricture, as, for example, when he describes "the tongue of man" as "a trumpet of war and sedition" (EW, II, 67). Such a phrase acquires authority from a metaphorical use of words in a way that departs from their proper meaning.

Although it would be illuminating to enumerate all of the changes which Hobbes makes in *De Cive,* it is only possible to suggest some of the more important ones. In chapter six, "On the Right of Him, Whether Council or One Man Only, Who Hath the Supreme Power in the City," Hobbes does not assert bluntly, as he does in the comparable chapter in *The Elements of Law,* that "the wills of most men are governed by fear" (II, 2, 6). Instead, the statement is supported by an appeal to experience and common knowledge, an appeal so evident as to assume almost the force of an aphorism: "for the pravity of human disposition is manifest to all, and by experience too well known how little (removing the punishment) men are kept to their duties through conscience of their promises" (EW, II, 75).

Still another example of how Hobbes appeals to experience occurs in section eight of chapter six, which corresponds to part two, chapter two, of *The Elements of Law*. Both are occupied with the essential indivisibility of the executive and judicial powers in the sovereign. The earlier version depends upon a compressed logical argument to the effect that "seeing to have the right of the sword, is nothing else but to have the use thereof depending only on the judgment and discretion of him or them that have it." In *De Cive* a similar statement is followed by an additional three sentences which depend for their effect upon an appeal to common sense: "for if the power of judging were in one, and the power of executing were in another, nothing would be done. For in vain would he give judgment, who could not execute his commands, or, if he executed them by the power of another, he himself is not said to have the power of the sword, but that other, to whom he is only an officer" (EW, II, 76–77). The sense of irresistible logic in this passage comes from Hobbes's control of parallelism and emphasis. Through this parallelism and emphasis, Hobbes seeks to convey the impression that the doctrine of mixed sovereignty is so inherently absurd as to require almost no discussion.

Hobbes's increasing willingness to go beyond logic in addressing his audience is perhaps illustrated most clearly in chapter eight, "Of the Rights of Lords over their Servants." In place of a bland statement introducing a section on men in the state of nature in *The Elements of Law,* Hobbes inserts a memorable formulation which has been as widely quoted as any passage in *De Cive:* "Let us return again to the state of nature, and consider men as if but even now sprung out of the earth, and suddenly, like mushrooms, come to full maturity, without all kind of engagement to each other" (EW, II, 108–109). This appeal to the reader's imagination is perfectly appropriate to Hobbes's view of the state of nature. Far more effectively than direct statement, the metaphor and accompanying explanatory simile demonstrate the complete removal of the state of nature from historical actuality. This opening establishes a convincing context for Hobbes's subsequent argument: no other phrase could be more effective in showing the origin of dominion unencumbered by historical circumstance.

In chapter eleven, Hobbes combines material covered in chapters six and seven of part two of *The Elements of Law* concerning places in scripture supportive of Hobbes's doctrine. Since Hobbes deals with the relation of church and state in part three of *De Cive,* this chapter is greatly abbreviated. It does not attempt to deal with scriptural evidence for his thought in systematic fashion but rather offers a sampling of passages that might be cited in support of isolated aspects of his political theory. By far the most interesting of these quotations is a passage from Judges 17:6: "In those days there was no king in Israel: every man did that which was right in his own eyes." Hobbes introduces this statement as proof of his central proposition that without a supreme power there is no government but anarchy. Although scriptural quotations are not being treated here as the main foundation of Hobbes's political theory, this chapter shows that they could effectively be used to confirm his propositions.

The differences between *The Elements of Law* and *De Cive* are apparent not only in short passages but in longer sections as well. An important example is Hobbes's treatment of tyrannicide in chapter twelve, "The Internal Causes of Dissolution." Hobbes's approach is basically the same in both works but where his tone in *The Elements of Law* (II, 8, 10) is cool and logical, his attitude in *De Cive* is entirely different. Abandoning his pose of philosophical detachment, he is nonetheless able to invoke an ironic perspective, to place the issue against a cosmic background:

But he whom men require to be put to death as being a *tyrant,* commands either by right or without right. If without right, he is an enemy, and by right to be put to death; but then this must not be called the *killing a tyrant,* but an *enemy.* If by right, then the divine interrogation takes place: *Who hath told thee that he was a tyrant? Hast thou eaten of the tree, whereof I commanded thee that thou shouldst not eat?* For why dost thou call him a *tyrant*, whom God hath made a *king*, except that thou, being a private person, usurpest to thyself the knowledge of *good* and *evil?* But how pernicious this opinion is to all government, but especially to that which is *monarchical,* we may hence discern; namely, that by it every king, whether good or ill, stands exposed to be the judgment, and slain by the hand of every murderous villain. (EW, II 153)

Without falling to the temptation of an emotional outburst, Hobbes manages to convey effectively a sense of indignation. The rhetoric seems carefully calculated, especially in the sharp reversal — indicated by the conjunction "but" — from irony to explicit judgment, and in the carefully controlled climax rising to a peak in the closing phrase of the paragraph. Every word seems calculated to achieve the maximum persuasive effect.

It should be emphasized that the principal appeal of *De Cive* is rational and argumentative. Hobbes still desired to achieve what he described in *The Elements of Law* as "the rules and infallibility of reason," but a reason now tempered by passion: Hobbes insists that he does not want to follow the example of the masters of rhetoric whose aim "is not truth (except by chance) but victory; and whose propriety is not to inform but to allure" (EW, II, 138). Nevertheless, as Hobbes well knew, if the reader's understanding was to be affected, then he had to be kept in touch with the realities which Hobbes's propositions signified. Metaphor, simile, allusion, analogue, all based upon an appeal to experience — these then become acceptable. Some examples of this appeal have already been illustrated; a further instance occurs in a discussion in chapter twelve on the imaginary discontents of subjects: "For they suffer the same thing with them who have a disease they call an *incubus;* which springing from gluttony, it makes men believe they are invaded, oppressed, and stifled with a great weight" (EW, II, 159). What is distinctive about Hobbes's use of analogy here is the way in which it becomes not merely ornament but part of the argument. That the appetites are the source of sedition is the thesis that Hobbes is urging — and it is to the rational implication in the simile that attention must be given. Thus, the aim of the analogy is not to inflame the passions but to inspire an ironic detachment.

Such a view of the significance of the imagery in *De Cive* seems confirmed by the powerful concluding passage of chapter twelve:

For *folly* and *eloquence* concur in the subversion of government, in the same manner (as the fable hath it) as heretofore the daughters of Pelias, king of Thessaly, conspired with Medea against their father. They going to restore the decrepit old man to his youth again, by the counsel of Medea they cut him into pieces, and set him in the fire to boil; in vain expecting when he would live again. So the common people, through their folly, like the daughters of Pelias, desiring to renew the ancient government, being drawn away by the *eloquence* of ambitious men, as it were by the witchcraft of Medea; divided into *faction* they consume it rather by those flames, than they reform it. (EW, II, 164)

Here, too, the argument is animated by analogy: folly and eloquence lead to remedies which are the reverse of what reason
demands. The vision of the final dissolution of "the ancient
government" by flames is given the inevitability of classical fable.
Hobbes apparently feels no need of further explanation or justification; his analogy is unqualified. He offers without further
comment an image of destruction so final as to become an ironic
horror.

The intention of this mode of reasoning is to unite eloquence and
wisdom. The contrast at the heart of Hobbes's polemics in *De Cive*
is not between rhetoric and logic but between an irresponsible
rhetoric and a rhetoric that is logically rigorous. He assumes that
"eloquence is twofold," and that one can distinguish between the
two parts: "The one is an elegant and clear expression of the
conceptions of the mind; and riseth partly from the contemplation
of the things themselves, partly from an understanding of words
taken in their proper and definite signification. The other is a
commotion of the passions of the mind, such as are *hope, fear,
anger, pity;* and derives from a metaphorical use of words fitted to
the passions" (EW, II, 161–162). Far from severing eloquence from
wisdom, Hobbes thinks that true eloquence is "never disjoined
from wisdom." The eloquence that Hobbes proposes will serve the
understanding by explaining "things as they are" and by forming
speech from "true principles," to achieve an end "truth" rather
than "victory."

The last chapter of "Dominion" in *De Cive,* like the last chapter
of *De Corpore Politico* in *The Elements of Law,* is concerned with
Hobbes's theory of law. Both chapters express the same viewpoint,
but Hobbes's treatment of that viewpoint is much more emphatic
in *De Cive* than in *The Elements of Law* and therefore deserves
closer attention. The first section of chapter fourteen shows that
"counsel" and "law" must be sharply opposed. Since "counsel" is
given to the "willing," while "law" is given to the "unwilling,"
"law" belongs to whoever "hath power" over them to whom it is
administered, even though it also contains within it "reason of its
obedience" (EW, II, 183). Inasmuch as the laws of nature are unen-
forceable in the state of nature, it follows that in reality they must
have the state of counsels; that is, they are precepts in which the
reason of our obeying them is taken from "the thing itself which is
advised" (EW, II, 183). By contrast, civil laws are a human crea-

tion that can replace the laws of nature but only when precept is combined with power.

Hobbes makes a similar distinction between law and covenant in section two. He insists that only covenants have their origin in the consent of men. For if laws were based upon consent, they could be nothing but "weak and naked contracts" that can be altered at our "will and pleasure." To clarify this distinction Hobbes added in a footnote that "a man is obliged by his contracts, that is, that he ought to perform for his promise sake; but that the law ties him being obliged, that is to say, it compels him to make good his promise for fear of the punishment appointed by the law" (EW, II, 185). A subject therefore has only one fundamental political obligation in the strict sense; to keep his promise to obey the sovereign. By virtue of this obligation, however, he is also commanded to obey the civil laws. In this way civil laws take on the character of both covenant and law. Because a subject who disobeys a civil law may obviously succeed, his action is unjust rather than imprudent. In the deepest sense, it is a form of rebellion against the sovereign, which Hobbes regards as a transgression of natural rather than civil law: "if some sovereign prince should set forth a law on this manner, *thou shalt not rebel*, he would effect just nothing. For except subjects were before obliged to obedience, that is to say, not to rebel, all law is of no force" (EW, II, 201). Hobbes seems to imply here that fear of punishment is ultimately insufficient to compel obedience, without a prior promise of compliance.

In order to make obedience certain, Hobbes appears to overlook a distinction between common rights and private rights which he made earlier in *De Cive*. In chapter three he had asserted that although men have equal right to all things in the state of nature, they can acquire and retain certain private rights: the right to use fire, water, air, space, and whatever private rights they are also willing to allow others (EW, II, 39–40). In chapter fourteen, however, Hobbes appears to deny that men may have private rights in the state of nature. He insists that since nature has given every man the right to all things, the precepts of the decalogue, by which man is forbidden to invade the rights of others, must be civil laws not laws of nature (EW, II, 189).[9] This stipulation is important because if civil laws which "forbid theft, adultery, etc." do not have a natural origin, they cannot be used by the subject as a basis upon which to judge the civil laws of the sovereign. All traditions concerning the identity of civil laws and natural laws are therefore useless and without foundation and it becomes virtually impossible for the sovereign to command anything by the civil law contrary to the laws of nature: "For though the law of nature forbid theft, adultery, etc.; yet if the civil law command us to invade anything, that invasion is not theft, adultery, etc. For when the Lacedaemonians of old permitted their youths, by a certain law, to take away other men's goods, they commanded that these goods should not be accounted other men's, but their own who took them; and therefore such surreptions were no thefts. In like manner, copulations of heathen sexes, according to their laws, were lawful marriages" (EW, II, 191). In this way, the principle of common rights in the state of nature establishes a fundamental distinction between natural law and civil law; the laws of nature are everywhere the same, but civil laws may vary considerably from one society to another.

3. *"Religion"*

Part three of *De Cive,* for which there is no corresponding part in *The Elements of Law,* is composed of four chapters: "Of the Kingdom of God by Nature," "Of His Government by the Old Covenant," "Of His Government By the New Covenant," and "Of Those Things which are Necessary for our Entrance in the Kingdom of Heaven." Although much of the material of these chapters can be found in different parts of *The Elements of Law* (e.g., I, 11; II, 6; II, 7), it is set forth here in a systematic and comprehensive manner. The function of "Religion" in *De Cive* is to define the relationship between church and state. As Hobbes himself posed the issue: "There is one thing only wanting to the complete understanding of all civil duty, and that is, to know which are the laws and commandments of God. For else we cannot tell whether that which the civil power commands us, be against the laws of God, or not; whence it must necessarily happen, that either by too much obedience to the civil authority, we become stubborn against the divine Majesty; or for fear of sinning against God, we run into disobedience against the civil power" (EW, II, 204).

Because Hobbes approached the subject of religion in *De Cive* with the aim of avoiding controversy, he was careful not to identify the religious groups whose views he was opposing. Yet Hobbes was clearly addressing two contrasting extremes. One extreme was represented by the Puritans, who held that private conscience —

the inner light — provided by itself a necessary justification for obedience entirely apart from church and state. The other extreme was represented by a minority in the Catholic Church who, Hobbes supposed, "believe themselves bound to acquiesce to a foreign authority in those doctrines which are necessary to salvation" (EW, II, 294).

Hobbes opposed both positions. He emphatically denied that the individual conscience could justify disobedience to the established church; he also denied that there is a universal church apart from the state. Within the commonwealth, the source under God of all authority and justification, and the interpreter of scripture is the Christian sovereign. In its emphasis upon the coexistence of church and state, this position bears at least a connection to the mainstream of tradition in the Church of England. But it departs from Anglican doctrine in its rigorous subordination of church to state.

As the foundation of his defense of this position, Hobbes turned in chapter fifteen to an exposition of the role which natural reason shares with "immediate revelation" and "prophecy" in providing the basis for religious faith. Of the three grounds of belief, Hobbes virtually excludes the second — visions, dreams, voices, divine inspiration — because "God's *sensible word* hath come but to few" and no "laws of his kingdom have been published on this manner unto any people" (EW, II, 206). These limitations are not true, however, of reason; Hobbes points out that there are some basic truths of religion which can be discovered by reason alone. These truths include the existence and attributes of God (EW, II, 213–216), the proper forms of divine worship (EW, II, 216–219), and the duties of men to one another, which, according to Hobbes, are "only the *natural laws*, namely, those which we have set down in chapters two and three' (EW, II, 210). Together, they constitute natural religion which is wholly prior to and independent of divine revelation.

By incorporating divine worship into natural religion, Hobbes opposed Puritans who made this a matter of special revelation. He argued that while some "*names* and *appellations*" are "always signs of scorn," "infinite others . . . are indifferent" (EW, II, 220). Hence, inasmuch as Hobbes had already shown how "every subject hath transferred as much right as he could on him or them who had the supreme authority," every subject could also have "transferred his right of judging the manner of how God is to be honoured; and therefore also he hath done it" (EW, II, 221).

It was nonetheless necessary that God make revelation to mankind. In the first place, reason is not the only element in natural religion; for Hobbes, there is also fear which stems from man's awareness of his own natural "weakness," that he has not a sufficient protection in himself. Moreover, the use of reason was "imperfect," beclouded by the "violence of the passions" so that it was impossible for man to worship God aright. Out of this limitation arose two errors: superstition — "fear without right reason" — and "atheism" — "an opinion of right reason without fear" (EW, II, 227). As the corrective of these errors, "it pleased the Divine Majesty ... to call forth Abraham, by whose means he might bring men to the true worship of him" (EW, II, 227).

At this point in his argument, Hobbes reveals another cause of revelation, a cause older than natural religion by far and perhaps ultimately irreconcilable with it, the fall of man. As his account makes clear, the fall of man is central to the Hobbesian body politic. God's Kingdom over man before the fall originated not "naturally" but by covenant, "that is to say, by the consent of the men themselves" (EW, II, 228). In God's kingdom, obedience was required without "dispute whether that were *good* or *evil* which was commanded." God's special commandment was the precept "of not eating of the tree of *the knowledge of good and evil.*" It was the desire to rival God in the knowledge of good and evil that caused the fall of man, and as a consequence of the fall, man has gained the illusion of good and evil. The distinguishing feature of this explanation is that good becomes identified as such and is put into operation only after man has lost his natural innocence. Because natural innocence knows no distinction between good and evil, it willingly covenants to accept the commandments of God without question. The fruits of the fall are thus the endless controversies and disputes concerning meum and tuum, right and wrong, etc., that prevent human beings from living amicably with one another. Abraham thus becomes for Hobbes the prototype of the sovereign. Since he was "the *interpreter* of all *laws,* as well sacred as secular ... it follows, that Abraham's subjects could not sin in obeying him" (EW, II, 230–231).

But if revelation provided man with a model for a religious commonwealth, it provided little else that was not already embodied in natural religion. Indeed, Hobbes goes so far as to insist that in the Kingdom of God under the Old Covenant "we read of no laws given by God to Abraham ... excepting the commandment of *circumcision,* which is contained in the covenant itself. Whence it is manifest, that there are no other laws or worship, which Abraham was obliged to, but the laws of nature, rational worship, and circumcision" (EW, II, 230).[9] Hobbes develops a similar argument in chapter seventeen," Of the Kingdom of God under the New Covenant." Of the two precepts of Christ (Matthew xx, 37-40), the "first was given before by Moses in the same words (Deut. vi. 5); and the second even before Moses; for it is the natural law, having its begining with rational nature itself; and both together is the sum of all laws" (EW, II, 264).

The net result of this Hobbesian natural religion was to make the sovereign the head of the Christian church. Since Christ has no other laws "beside the institution of the sacrament of *baptism* and the *eucharist"* (EW, II, 264), it follows that the subject is obliged to obey the sovereign in all temporal matters. Inasmuch as both church and state (which Hobbes calls a city in *De Cive*) are formed by the lawful assembly of a multitude, a state of Christian men can be called a church. Within a Christian state the interpretation of scripture — that is, the right of settling spiritual controversies — thus devolves upon the temporal sovereign (EW, II, 278, 294-295). Hobbes is careful to preserve an important but minor place in this scheme for the clergy; it is empowered to settle questions concerning "mysteries of faith," to remit sins, and to elect churchmen.

In chapter eighteen, concerning the articles of faith necessary for salvation, Hobbes attempts to establish a foundation upon which a Christian subject might plausibly accept the authority of a secular sovereign (or more important, the sovereign of another faith) in spiritual matters. This concern prompts Hobbes to define an object of religious faith in chapter eighteen not as an idea but as "a *proposition,* that is to say, a speech affirmative or negative which we grant to be true" (EW, II, 302). By thus reducing faith to rational assent, Hobbes could insist that if assent "were necessarily required to the truth of all and each proposition, which this day is controverted about the Christian faith, or by divers churches is diversely defined; there would be nothing more difficult for the Christian religion" (EW, II, 309-310). Because such unanimity is obviously impossible, Hobbes argues that "only one article, that

Jesus is the Christ" is "necessary for salvation." But how does this article become an object of religious faith? Since faith is defined as "trust in another man's knowledge," Hobbes's answer to this question is that "to believe in Christ ... is nothing else but to believe Jesus himself, saying that he is the Christ" (EW, II, 306).

Although incomplete, this summary suggests how Hobbes's position came to be so easily misunderstood. His theory of church and state differs both from the tradition of a Christian commonwealth founded upon the supremacy of the church in spiritual matters and from the modern alternative of a secular state based upon the separation of the two powers. It is the theory of a philosopher who sought to subordinate church to state, but it is also the theory of a man who wished to preserve the essential features of a Christian commonwealth. The assumption that church can be subordinated to state and that a Christian commonwealth can be preserved may be incompatible ideals. However, Hobbes's attempt to reconcile these two disparate ideals engendered the distinguishing and novel features of his account: the derivation of the principles of a secular commonwealth from scriptures; the restriction of revelation to the institution of rites and sacraments; the ascription of spiritual powers to a temporal authority; and the reduction of the articles of faith required for salvation to an irreducible minimum.

# Leviathan

IT is, of course, for *Leviathan* that Hobbes is chiefly remembered in the twentieth century, even among people with little interest in philosophy. After 1667, it was not reissued in a separate edition until 1884. In our own time, however, *Leviathan* has been reissued in numerous formats ranging from inexpensive paperbacks to deluxe collectors' editions. There have been three full-length studies devoted exclusively to it,[1] and it has always occupied the central position in more general works on Hobbes's political thought.

Probably nothing, however, has brought Hobbes's work so much to the attention of a large public as the fact that its title has passed into popular nomenclature. Leviathan, as an allusion to the sea monster who rules as "king over all the children of pride" (41:34) in the Book of Job, seems lively and singularly relevant to readers who have little or no knowledge of scripture or of civil philosophy. Although the term is often used by many who have no awareness of its biblical origin or of Hobbes's application of it, it has undoubtedly led others back to Hobbes's work, to discover in Leviathan an answer to man's political dilemmas with all their confusions and uncertainties. In the sense that it conveys of the awesome power of civil government, Hobbes's *Leviathan* appears to speak directly to our time.

In its own time, *Leviathan* was often searched for its political implications, but its connection with current politics is much less straightforward than might be supposed. By some contemporaries, it was believed to have been written to defend Stuart absolutism; by others, it was thought to "flatter" Oliver Cromwell, the acknowledged enemy of the Stuarts. It was described as a denunciation of kings in general and of Charles II in particular. More specifically, its publication in 1651 gave rise to the suspicion that its purpose was to justify the King's party, which had given into parliament after the Battle of Worcester when the King's cause was perceived as hopeless.[2] Royalist conservatives later found it tainted by the radical doctrine of the Levellers and accused Hobbes of being a cynical betrayer of the English aristocracy. In more recent times, one critic has discovered in it a reflection of Marxist historical assumptions concerning England in the seventeenth century,[3] while another has described its politics as basically medieval, Christian, and scriptural in the orthodox sense.[4]

It seems certain that Hobbes himself was not aware of any specific political motives in composing *Leviathan*. His general aim was undoubtedly the same as it had been in *The Elements of Law* and in *De Cive;* he wanted *Leviathan* to have a practical effect, to instruct those in power in what he had learned about the nature and science of politics. Yet, leaving aside the question of the development of Hobbes's ideas, we can see that *Leviathan* differs considerably in its general attitude from its predecessors. Unlike *The Elements of Law* and *De Cive, Leviathan* does not conform to a conventional philosophic or educational genre: it is *sui generis. Leviathan* has often been characterized as a "popular" account of Hobbes's political doctrines, yet it is manifest from the way it departs from Hobbes's earlier standards of political discourse that he was no longer convinced of the possibility of erecting a system that would be above controversy as in *The Elements of Law* or even of minimizing the controversial aspects of that system as in *De Cive*. In spite of his commitment to his earlier educational ideals, Hobbes frequently couched his propositions in *Leviathan* in terms that were pungent, even shocking. The analogy between the sovereign power and leviathan, for example, was chosen for its originality and vividness. It enabled Hobbes to draw upon a traditional analogy: the comparison of the state to a human body. In *Leviathan,* that comparison occurs in a number of chapters as a (rather obvious) unifying thematic device. But Hobbes's application of leviathan, the seamonster, to the body politic was unconventional. The body politic is an "artificial" not a "natural" body; hence like artificial creations, it is not only mortal but is also subject to malfunctions and disorders that are humanly created (EW, III, ix–x).

This technique served Hobbes's new aim to disturb his readers, but it was also more in keeping with a mind naturally aware of ironies. In *Leviathan,* Hobbes consciously assumed the attitude of a publicist and partisan, adopting the Lucretian pose of a philospher who seeks to clear away the veils of superstition and ignorance from mankind. In the "Epistle Dedicatory" to Mr. Francis Godolphin, he makes quite clear his awareness that he will not have an easy time of it in certain quarters: "That which perhaps may most offend, are certain texts of Holy Scripture, alleged by me to other purposes than ordinarily they use to be by others. But I have done it with due submission, and also, in order to my subject necessarily; for they are the outworks of the enemy, from whence they impugn the civil power" (EW, III, v). Thus, Hobbes signifies his intention to persist and to no longer attempt to mitigate the implications of his ideas. His style in *Leviathan* is lively, his irony biting. Whether in his scathing analysis of false piety or in his attacks against the educational ideals of Oxford University, Hobbes increasingly resorted to a mode which magnified the weaknesses of his targets in order to turn them to ridicule. To his contemporaries, he was coming to be known as a man who delighted to assume the posture of the devil's advocate.

But if Hobbes freely indulged his gift for irony in *Leviathan,* it was because he was anxious to attract attention for his ideas. He continued to refine not only his basic argument but also his method. In the "Introduction" to *Leviathan,* Hobbes advanced beyond the simple appeal to experience of *De Cive.* In place of a reliance upon an observation of men in society, Hobbes substituted a more sophisticated notion of introspection:

... there is another saying not of late understood ... that is, *nosce teipsum, read thyself:* which was ... meant ... to teach us, that for the similitude of the thoughts and passions of one man, to the thoughts and passions of another, whosoever looketh into himself, and considereth what he doth, when he does *think, opine, reason, hope, fear,* &c. and upon what grounds; he shall thereby read and know, what are the thoughts and passions of all other men upon the like occasions. I say the similitude of *passions,* which are the same in all men, *desire, fear, hope* &c; which are the things *desired, feared, hoped,* &c: for these the constitution individual, and particular education do so vary, and they are so easy to be kept from our knowledge, that the characters of mans heart, blotted and confounded as they are with dissembling, lying, counterfeiting, and erroneous doctrines, are legible only to him that searcheth hearts. And though by men's actions we do discover their design sometimes; yet to do it without comparing them with our own, and distinguishing all circumstances, by which the case may come to be altered, is to decypher without a key, and be for the most part deceived, by too much trust, or by too much diffidence; as he that reads, is himself a good or evil man. (EW, III, xi–xii)

In this passage, the crucial point is that Hobbes no longer believed, as he did in *De Cive,* that it is possible for us to discover the "designs" of others by their "actions," Unless such an undertaking involves a comparison of our own natures with those of others, it would probably lead us to impose our own basic good or evil identities upon them, while concealing from ourselves the falsity of the information we would gain from this enterprise. It follows that simply by looking inward we can discover our "natural" passions, entirely apart from the way they are modified by our own "individual" constitutions or "particular" educational experiences, or from the way they are confounded by the dissembling, lying, and counterfeiting of others. In these terms, we can discover the "natural condition of man," that is his condition in the state of nature, without being influenced by the way he appears in society. There is one difficulty, however. In view of the variety of things men desire, how can we be certain of the "similitude of passions" in all men? But in light of the knowledge introspection is supposed to produce, this similitude would appear to be substantiated in Hobbes's opinion by the subsequent comparisons the knowledge we gain of ourselves enables us to make between ourselves and others.

It may be objected that this procedure merely substitutes a doubtful subjectivity for an uncertain objectivity. Hobbes's own contemporaries were not slow to charge that his "low" view of mankind was largely derived from his reading of his own ill-nature. Whatever its limitations, however, this approach has the merit of reflecting the fundamental opposition in Hobbes's system of ideas between passion and reason, nature and society. Since Hobbes believes that reason brings us together and the passions (except fear) divide us, it follows that the only way to discover the nature of passions that are necessarily non-social is through self-analysis.

## I  *"Of Man"*

*Leviathan* is divided into four major parts. The first two, "Of

Man" and "Of Commonwealth," taking up about half the volume, correspond to the two sections of *The Elements of Law:
Human Nature,* and *De Corpore Politico.* The third part, "Of a
Christian Commonwealth," is a further development and expansion of the ideas set forth in part three, "Religion," in *De Cive.* A
fourth part, "Of the Kingdom of Darkness," which is entirely new,
is a stunning *tour de force* in which Hobbes draws upon the
rational method to expose the errors and superstitions that have
arisen in the past from misinterpretations of scripture, demonology, "vain philosophy and fabulous traditions."

The first three chapters of *Leviathan,* part one, dealing with the
mental faculties, parallel chapter two to four of *Human Nature* in
*The Elements of Law.* Although Hobbes preserves the basic postulates of his earlier account of mind, his treatment of them betrays a
measure of uneasiness. Perhaps the most obvious evidence of this
uneasiness is the instability in Hobbes's terminology. In chapter
one, "Of Sense," Hobbes retains the term "seeming" to refer to
sense impressions, but substitutes "fancy" for "apparition,"
which he now consigns to the rubbish heap of scholastic jargon,
along with "species" and other terms. In chapter two, "Of
Imagination," the word "memory" is introduced for the first time
as a synonym for the Latin term "imagination," which Hobbes
now refers to as an "image" rather than a "conception." Memory
is composed of images which are retained in the mind after the
objects presented to the senses are removed. Finally, in the third
chapter, in place of the word "discursion," by which Hobbes
meant a train of thoughts, he substitutes the word "mental discourse" apparently in order to avoid confusion with the phrase
"discourse in words."

These changes are not merely a quibble on words. They reveal a
crisis in terminology, as Hobbes struggled to draw from the vast,
seemingly inchoate jumble of scholastic terminology a few basic
terms which would define the various elements of the mind. An
indication of his awareness of the possibility of verbal anarchy is
revealed in his habit of using redundant word pairs joined by the
conjunctions "and" and "or" to indicate alternative names:
"desire and appetite," "consequence or train of thoughts," "seeming or fancy," "marks or notes," "image or fancy." The list could
easily be multiplied. On whatever subject, Hobbes was searching
for the right names to make his ideas clear. In fact the importance

of Hobbes's treatment of mind for the history of philosophy may lie as much in his attempt to clear away the philosophical jargon of the past as in his effort to formulate a new theory of knowledge. The energy he expended on terminology illustrates how far from obvious the terms were and how formidable the problems to be solved.

This concern for words may have led Hobbes to alter the attitude of these chapters. In *Leviathan,* speech, which Hobbes calls "the most noble and profitable invention of all other," grows in importance at the expense of the senses, memory, and imagination, as Hobbes lays stress upon the active aspect of speech and the passive element of the other faculties. Reference to "remembrance" as a "sixth sense," by which we take note of our conceptions, drops out of the argument of the chapter on memory, and Hobbes chooses instead to speak only of the passive reproduction of images. In a similar way, his revised analysis of sense impressions still leaves intact the conviction that physical reality is quite different from the world of appearances which exist in man's own mind. In effect, Hobbes widens the gap between the "five senses" and man's "other faculties." The former required "no other thing, to the exercise" of them, "but to be born a man." The latter, on the other hand, require strenuous attention: "Those other faculties, of which I shall speak by and by, and which seem proper to man only, are acquired, and increased by study and industry ... and proceed all from the invention of words, and speech" (EW, III, 16).

Without speech, Hobbes goes on to suggest, "there had been amongst men, neither commonwealth, nor society, nor contract, nor peace, no more than amongst lions, bears, and wolves" (EW, III, 18). For the first time, Hobbes identifies the passage from nature to society with the invention of speech rather than with the institution of a common power to overawe us all. It is a natural corollary of Hobbes's pessimism that lacking speech, which is associated with reason, human beings are to be reckoned more like solitary animals of prey than animals who come together peacefully in herds and cells. Man is more like a wolf or a bear than he is like a cow or a bee.

Occupying an intermediate status between passive mental states and the active, conscious discipline of speech is what Hobbes calls "trains of thought." As an axiom of *The Elements of Law,* Hobbes had stated that thought by itself did not distinguish man from beasts (I, 5, 1). Now in chapter three of *Leviathan* Hobbes observes that of the mental activity of imagining how many effects can be produced by a thing "I have not at any time seen any sign, but in man only; for this is a curiosity hardly incident to the nature of any living creature that has no other passion but sensual, such as are hunger, thirst, lust, and anger" (EW, III, 13–14). According to Hobbes, all "coherent thought" is "regulated by some desire and design." The two words are not exactly identical, the latter implying a greater degree of conscious motivation than the former.

To distinguish between two kinds of coherent thought, Hobbes applied the idea of cause and effect. In the first kind, we explain how something comes to be, that is "of an effect imagined, we seek the causes, or means that produce it: and this is common to man and beast" (EW, III, 13). In the second, which is common to men alone, we explain something by identifying what it can do: "when imagining anything whatsoever, we seek all the possible effects, that can by it be produced, that is to say, we imagine what we can do with it, when we have it" (EW, III, 13). In both cases, the implicit model for mental activity when it is governed by "desire and design" is the hunting dog. In order to trace the configurations of mental activity, Hobbes also applies this model in two ways. As a search for something lost, it is a movement backwards "from place to place, and time to time, to find when and where he had it"; and then a doubling back in which the "runs over the same places and times, to find what action, or other occasion might make him lose it" (EW, III, 14). As a search from "a place determinate, within the compass whereof he is to seek," the mind's activity resembles the sweeping "of a room, to find a jewel," or the ranging "of a field" to discover a scent, or the running over the alphabet, to discover a rhyme (EW, III, 14). These configurations are important, because mental activity viewed as animal impulsion is a non-rational substitute for the traditional concept of memory as an active, rational faculty. Mental activity which involves selective recall and retrieval is dissociated from memory which is occupied with the storage of images.

In one respect, which was of immense importance for the future development of English empirical psychology, Hobbes explored new ground in his account of mental thought in chapter three. In *The Elements of Law,* Hobbes had explained the cause of the coherence of our thoughts by suggesting that they occur in our minds in the same order in which they originally appeared to our senses (I, 4, 2). In order to emphasize the importance of desire in "regulated thought," Hobbes relegates this explanation to the subordinate status of "unregulated thought" in *Leviathan*. "To one and the same thing perceived," he now writes, "sometimes one thing, sometimes another succeedeth." As a consequence, "there is no certainty what we shall imagine next" (EW, III, 12). It is clear from the entire discussion that Hobbes no longer regards this principle as a cause of coherence. Rather he frames his discussion on implicit considerations of association. The passage is of interest as a groping effort toward what later British empiricists were to call "association by contiguity." Similarly, in a discussion of "unguided thoughts," to which Hobbes devotes a new section, he stressed that their ordering is not entirely fortuitous: "in this wild-ranging of the mind, a man may oft-times perceive the way of it, and the dependence of one thought upon another" (EW, III, 12). The subsequent illustration of the "value of a Roman penny" contains the first explicit discussion of association by resemblance in the history of philosophy. The development of the laws of association demanded a further exploration of the path Hobbes opened in this chapter.

These points, however, despite their importance, are merely a prelude to Hobbes's forceful and lengthy presentation of his theory of speech in chapter four. This theory is essentially rational: speech consists "of *names* or *appelations,* and their connexion; whereby men register their thoughts; recall them when they are past; and also declare them one to another for mutual utility and conversation" (EW, III, 18). The general purpose of speech is "to transfer our mental discourse into verbal or [to transfer] the train of our thoughts, into a train of words" (EW, III, 19). Considered in relation to Hobbes's conception of speech as an activity which is sharply distinguished from thought, Hobbes's insistence that *"true* and *false* are attributes of speech, not of things" becomes comprehensible. What he believed with increasing conviction was that "in the right definition of names lies the first use of speech; which is the acquisition of science; and in wrong, or no definitions, lies the first abuse, from which proceed all false and senseless tenets" (EW, III, 24). The beginning of knowledge, therefore, is an examination of "the definitions" of former authors. To facilitate this examination, Hobbes introduced a section which offered criteria for the use and abuse of words. Characteristically, semantic and ethical considerations are entwined in Hobbes's discussion of the four abuses. The first occurs when men use words without any clear idea of their meanings and "so deceive themselves." The second occurs when men use words metaphorically, in another sense than they were intended for and "so deceive others." The third when men use words to "declare that to be their will, which is not"; the fourth, when they "use them to grieve another." In this way, the use of words becomes a moral activity for Hobbes.

The most distinctive and important result of Hobbes's dichotomy between thought and speech was his nominalism. According to Hobbes, names are either proper to one thing or are common to many things. The latter, which are called "universal" names, are, as J.W.N. Watkins has aptly said, a "sort of pluralized version of proper names."[5] That is, universals are predicated of names, not of objects designated by these names. For while Hobbes believes that names may be universal, he also assumes that nothing exists in the world except particular things. Since all knowledge comes from experience, our "ideas of things" must also be "individual and singular" (EW, III, 21). This contrast between "ideas" and "names" corresponds, in the logic of Hobbes's argument, to the contrast between thought and speech. The argument is that ideas resemble the things they represent, while names do not look like or sound like what they signify. Ideas describe, names explain. Ideas individuate, that is they represent things to us as individuals; universal names classify; they explain things by properties (which Hobbes calles "accidents") which may be shared by many individual things. For Hobbes words are not iconic; they are arbitrary marks which "signify" our names and to which we attach definitions.

Yet, while words are arbitrary, they have meaning only by corresponding to specific ideas. Purely verbal thinking is, in Hobbes's opinion, a very dangerous activity. There is also the concern that once we lose sight of the ideas, we may fall into the error of using words in such a way that they do not correspond to ideas at all. When this phenomenon occurs, as Hobbes believes it often does, our thoughts become empty and meaningless. Yet, since words do not represent ideas in the same way that ideas represent things, they do not individuate as ideas do. If Hobbes is justified in making this distinction, then quite clearly what happens in speech is that a universal name will refer to many things at once, at the same time that it brings to mind an image of only "one of these many" things.

But is he justified? One worry is that Hobbes may have developed his nominalism to fit a mathematical model of human speech. Even if we were to accept his contention that things in themselves are individual, we might still wonder if his theory allows for the fact that, while the marks or symbols used by mathematicians do not look like or sound like what they signify — the number three doesn't look like three apples or three slices of pie — words or names used in everyday speech, even universal words or names, are often heavily loaded with sensory or imagistic values. Consequently such factors as iconicity and onomatopoeia may tend to blur the dichotomy between general names and particular ideas. Hobbes's distinction may not necessarily be invalid, but it may be less simple or less absolute than he seems to suggest.

In chapter five, mathematics is seen as the model for human reasoning: "When a man *reasoneth*, he does nothing else but conceive a sum total, from *addition* of *parcels;* or conceive a remainder, from *subtraction* of one sum from another; which, if it be done by words, is conceiving of the consequence of the names of all the parts, to the name of the whole; or from the names of the whole and one part, to the name of the other part" (EW, III, 29). Basic to his procedure here is the insight, first set forth in *The Elements of Law,* that words can be considered as arbitrary marks for the assistance of the memory, which, as we have seen, Hobbes regards as altogether deficient by itself for the tasks of everyday life. Thus, a word can be said to "register" a thought, in the same way that marks are used to register "notations" in ledger books. The most evident application of this principle is numbering. Without words, we will be unable even to "add, and subtract, and perform all other operations of arithmetic" (EW, III, 23). From this, Hobbes concluded that mathematics itself was a model for human reasoning. And yet although he employs mathematical language, we must not think that the mode of reasoning presented in *Leviathan* is solely based upon the Euclidean model of geometry. The examples which Hobbes cites are as much arithmetic as geometric in method and expression. For Hobbes's aim evidently was to extend the form of mathematical reasoning to all modes of thought. The simple calculations of arithmetic were perhaps better suited than the rigorous deductions of geometry to the reasoning of the ordinary person. A man does not have to be a natural philosopher to engage in "reckoning" as Hobbes describes it in *Leviathan*. But the final result of this enterprise is not entirely satisfactory. The extent to which Hobbes's new conception of reasoning may have induced others to apply mathematics to the problems of every day life cannot be shown. It is safe to say, however, that later practitioners of this method were tempted to lapse into a crude utilitarianism exemplified, for example, in the novels of Daniel Defoe where the mental calculations of the principle characters are conceived, in the words of one recent critic, in terms of "numbers, measures, cash values."⁶

At the same time, however, if we are to fully comprehend Hobbes's conception of thought and speech, we must recognize the presence of non-utilitarian elements in it. Unlike John Locke, Hobbes finds positive value in thoughts which are "unguided, without design." We make them "not only without company, but without care of anything" (EW, III, 12); and if Hobbes's illustration of the "Roman penny" is any indication, they can yield insight denied to rational thought. Of the four uses of speech, the last is "to please and delight ourselves and others, by playing with our words, for pleasure or ornament, innocently" (EW, III, 20).

In chapter five, "Of Reason and Science," Hobbes develops the implications of his conception of reasoning for science. The mark of scientific procedure is the deduction of the consequences of affirmations. The latter in turn are based upon "first definitions and settled significations of names" (EW, III, 31). Definitions are the sole basis for demonstration, "for there can be no certainty of the last conclusion, without a certainty of all those affirmations and negations, on which it was grounded and inferred." Since Hobbes demands that philosophical questions be posed in logical, deductive terms rather than in empirically inductive terms, he tends to regard errors in investigation which he calls "causes of absurdity," not as mistakes in the classification or interpretation of empirical data, but as violations of rules governing deductive reasoning, as, for example, beginning an argument without first settling the significations of definitions. Six additional causes of absurdity are listed in chapter five, but I omit them for the sake of brevity. As in mathematics, what matters for Hobbes are not the names themselves but the relations between them. In essence, Hobbes's method consists of isolating and accurately naming formal properties and of stating their necessary relations in the form of logical deductions. Hobbes describes this procedure as follows: "reason is ... attained by industry; first in apt imposing of names; and secondly by getting a good and orderly method of proceeding from the elements, which are names, to assertions made by connexion of one of them to another; and so to syllogisms, which are the connexions of one assertion to another, till we come to a knowledge of all the consequences of names appertaining to the subject in hand; and that is it, men call SCIENCE" (EW, III, 35).

Of the next eight chapters, the seventh, "On the Ends or Resolution in Discourse," and the ninth, "On the severall Subjects of knowledge," present little that is new; they are primarily a restatement and amplification of Hobbes's notions of opinion, knowledge, conscience, and science. The other chapters, however, represent a substantial revision of Hobbes's conception of human nature. Chapter six is concerned with the passions; chapter eight with wit, dullness, and madness; chapter ten, with power, worth, and honour; chapter eleven with desire and fear; chapter twelve, with the origin of religion; and chapter thirteen, with the natural condition of mankind. Hence they are of the greatest interest to students of Hobbes.

Compared to the equivalent analysis in *The Elements of Law* (I, 7-9), Hobbes's discussion of the passions in chapter six of *Leviathan* is considerably abbreviated and drastically revised. In the earlier treatise, the passions are seen as a manifestation of power, and in contrast to external passions, the internal emotion of glory occupies the preeminent place. In the revised version, power is disengaged from the passions and given separate treatment in chapter ten. In the process, glory is relegated to a subordinate position as simply one among a plurality of passions. Total elimination of power was impossible, however, since the analysis depended upon the premise that the passions arise from our desires and aversions, and power is necessary to achieve our appetites. With power reduced to that minimal content, Hobbes reverted to a much more traditional analysis of the passions in *Leviathan*.

The extent to which Hobbes's treatment of the passions in *Leviathan* differs from that of *The Elements of Law* becomes apparent from the following comparison. In the earlier treatise, Hobbes had explained the passions with reference to "vital motion." If motion "about the heart" increases vital motion, delight results; if it diminishes vital motion, pain results:

| *love* | delight with reference to an object |
| *hate* | pain with reference to an object |
| *good* | what we call the object of our desires |
| *evil* | what we call the object of our aversions |

Hobbes's subsequent classification of the passions arises from the perception of our power in relation to the power of others. This perception is not a certainty, but a subjective judgment we make about ourselves, in part, on the evidence of the appreciation of others. A partial list of passions in *The Elements of Law,* part one, chapter nine, can be summarized as follows:

| *glory* | imagination of our own power, above power of him that contendeth with us. |
| *false glory* | imagination of power above power of him that contendeth with us, ill grounded. |
| *vain glory* | imagination of power above power of him that contendeth with us, without endeavour. |
| *humility* | imagination of infirmity in rel. to a power of others, well grounded. |
| *dejection* | imagination of infirmity, ill grounded. |
| *shame* | remembrance of infirmity. |

The difficulty with this scheme is that, while it is bold and original, it is also unsystematic and inconsistent. It does not, for example, distinguish clearly between a present good which can only be presented to the senses and a future good which can only be presented to the imagination. In *Leviathan,* Hobbes overcame this difficulty by introducing an Aristotelian distinction between present and absent objects:

| *love* | presence of object, |
| *desire* | absence of object, |
| *hate* | presence of object, |
| *aversion* | absence of object, |
| *contempt* | object neither desired nor hated, |
| *good* | what we call the objects of our desire, |
| *evil* | what we call the objects of our aversion, |
| *pleasure* | appearance of good, |
| *displeasure* | appearance of evil, |
| *sensuality* | pleasures of sense, |
| *joy* | pleasures of mind |
| *pain* | displeasures of sense, |
| *grief* | displeasures of mind, |

As we have seen, Hobbes had already developed a distinction in *The Elements of Law* (Part One, Chapter Eight) between pleasures of sense and pleasures of mind, but he did not apply it consistently throughout his analysis of the passions. By differentiating between present and absent objects, Hobbes arrived in *Leviathan* at a view of pleasures of sense and pleasures of the mind which corresponds in many respects to a traditional separation of the concupiscible appetites whose object is sensible good and evil, from the irascible appetites, whose object is presented to the mind by reason.[7] Common to both *The Elements of Law* and *Leviathan* is Hobbes's belief that nothing is in itself universally good or evil, but takes on these characteristics according to whether it becomes the object of our desire or aversion. In this respect, Hobbes departs from all traditional theories which held that there are objective moral distinctions, with a foundation in the nature of things, which can be clearly apprehended by the individual. It is true that Hobbes's insistence upon the subjectivity of our perception of good and evil does not absolutely preclude the existence of objective moral distinctions.[8] Instead it tends to render the ability of the imagination to achieve certainty doubtful. An emphasis upon "seeming" good and "seeming" evil in *Leviathan* is the result.

The most striking instance of how Hobbes reverted in *Leviathan* to a more conventional treatment of the passions is his terse definition of "Benevolence, Good Will, Charity" as "desire of good to another" and of "GOOD NATURE" if this desire is directed "to man generally" (EW, III, 43). From the time of Bishop Butler it has generally been assumed that Hobbes's purpose in examining the passions was to construct an egoistic psychology, based upon a universal desire for power and fear of death. And yet if this is true of *The Elements of Law,* it is not true of *Leviathan.* As has recently been shown, such a view represents a misreading of Hobbes, similar to seventeenth century misconceptions about Epicurus and Machiavelli.[9] There is nothing in this passage to suggest that the passion of benevolence is egoistic. Hobbes's psychology has carried him back to an identification of charity with a concern for others — an identification he had appeared initially to deny.

In no sense, however, can it be said that Hobbes ever saw undiscriminated benevolence as a basis for forming civil society or as in some way "natural" to all men. Rather he approached benevolence as a desire which is neither prompted by innate goodness nor strictly governed by an inborn sense of good and evil. Moreover, desire is an affection and as such it is subject to change; thus, our present desire for good to others may not necessarily be translated into future action. Most important, however, Hobbes believed that to base a society upon benevolence is to put the cart before the horse. His clear distinction between the laws of nature and the actual behaviour of men led him to differ from benevolists on this crucial point. Hobbes maintains that the laws of nature are norms which people must obey not only in order to achieve peace but also to produce benevolence. Unless the law of gratitude is obeyed, "there will be no beginning of benevolence, or trust; nor consequently of mutual help; nor of reconciliation of one man to another" (EW, III, 138).

In chapter eight, Hobbes deals with wit, dullness, and madness. He begins by defining virtue as something "that is valued for its eminence; and consisteth in comparison" (EW, III, 56). There are two kinds of virtue "natural and acquired." Wit is a natural virtue, but that does not mean that wit is a virtue that man has had from birth, like his senses. Rather it is "gotten through use only and experience." Natural wit is thus defined in terms of a simple geometry of motion, in which the principle elements are *"celerity of imagining,* that is, swift succession of one thought to another, and *steady direction* to some approved end" (EW, III, 56). Consistent with this definition, "dullness" is no longer equated with sensuality as in *The Elements of Law* but with stupidity, understood as "slowness of motion, or difficulty to be moved" (EW, III, 56). On this basis Hobbes is able to establish a hierarchy of states of mind, based on different degrees of desire: "For as to have no desire, is to be dead: so to have weak passions, is dulness; and to have passions indifferently for every thing, GIDDINESS, and *distraction;* and to have stronger and more vehement passions for any thing, than is ordinarily seen in others, is that which men call MADNESS" (EW, III, 62).

In chapter ten, Hobbes treats power, "the present means, to obtain some future, apparent good." As in *The Elements of Law* Hobbes associates power with honor in *Leviathan.* To honor a man is to set a value on his power in relation to the value we set on our own power. In *Leviathan,* however, the analysis produces a significant redirection of the ultimate thrust of the argument. Although Hobbes began by characterizing honor in terms of such aristocratic norms as "value and worth," he shifts his ground in *Leviathan* by introducing the category of "price," with its connotations of trade and commerce:

The *value,* or WORTH of a man, is as of all other things, his price; that is to say, so much as would be given for the use of his power: and therefore is not absolute; but a thing dependent on the need and judgment of another. An able conductor of soldiers, is of great price in time of war present, or imminent; but in peace not so. A learned and uncorrupt judge, is much worth in time of peace; but not so much in war. And as in other things, so in men, not the seller, but the buyer determines the price. For let a man, as most men do, rate themselves at the highest value they can; yet their true value is no more than it is esteemed by others. (EW, III, 76)

Why does Hobbes seek to extend the meaning of honor to include price, using the analogy of buying and selling? Is his unconscious model, as C. B. Macpherson has suggested, the possessive market society, and is he a spokesman for a particular class without knowing it?[10] Or is his purpose merely rhetorical? Certainly, *Leviathan* represents Hobbes's most concerted effort to reach as wide an audience as possible. Yet Hobbes's analogy is more than a rhetorical figure of speech — it suggests that behind such values as honor, worth, and dignity is a world dominated by competitive display and envy, however reprehensible, and that the notion of a man's power as a commodity can be conscious and meaningful.

The appeal of the analogy of the marketplace to Hobbes may be in part due to his treatment of the word "honor." Hobbes's view of human nature entails as an assumption the moral indifference of the passions, even the passion of benevolence. Honor has become an external sign of power, whose value is no longer, even in part, a personal, interior quality related to the attainment of virtue and inseparable from its achievement. For Hobbes, honor is invariably used in the sense of external, public recognition, and moral virtue, which he identifies with the laws of nature, is independent of it. Honor thus becomes very similar to those virtues, natural and acquired, cited in chapter eight, which are derived from a comparison of the self to others. From this position, it is not very far to the view which invests worth with the primacy given by merchants to buying and selling. Divested of its inner moral qualities, honor is not unrelated to the ideal of competition embodied in a market society.

However, arguments of equal force can be marshalled for the view that Hobbes's ethos is still essentially aristocratic. Here too, the evidence is impressive and the connections illuminating. Almost all of the qualities which Hobbes enumerates as evidence of honor are aristocratic and heroic: "Riches, joined with liberality, is power; because it procureth friends, and servants: without liberality, no so; because in this case they defend not: but expose men to envy." And "magnanimity, liberality, hope, courage, confidence, are honourable; for they proceed from the conscience of power. Pusillanimity, parsimony, fear, diffidence, are dishonourable" (EW, III, 79). A large part of the chapter is devoted to "scutcheons and coats of arms hereditary" which Hobbes ascribes to a Germanic origin, and to "titles of honour." There is no corresponding attention given to bourgeois qualities, and the analogy of the marketplace seems to be explored most fully in Hobbes's analysis of contracts and covenants. Part of the problem confronting Hobbes in applying the model of commercial exchange to honor is the relative nature of judgments. As in *The Elements of Law,* the emphasis in *Leviathan* is not upon considerations of strategy: for instance, upon calculating the exact worth of our powers in seeking a job or negotiating a transaction. Rather it is based upon a judgment of past actions prompted by external acclamation. At this level honor seems, on the one hand, to be very close to male aggression displayed in certain animal species; on the other hand, it shows close affinities with public drama, acted out before the community as a whole. In competing for the applause of the spectators, the protagonists are required to exhibit liberality and magnificence, as indispensable accoutrements, in order to give credibility to their actions.[11]

In chapter eleven, "Of the difference in manners," Hobbes applies his generalized conception of power to "those qualities of man-kind, that concern their living together in peace, and unity." The chapter consists of an enumeration of the desires which dispose men "to obey a common power," and those which dispose them to "contention, enmity and war." Desire of ease, fear of death, fear of oppression, etc. incline men to obey a common power; competition of rights, vainglory, belief in our own wisdom, etc., incline men to contention. Although Hobbes's view is basically similar to that enunciated in *The Elements of Law*, he is able, by disengaging it from the ambiguities of his treatment of the passions, to give a bolder and more inclusive formulation: "So that in the first place, I put for a general inclination of all mankind, a perpetual and restless desire of power after power, that ceaseth only in death" (EW, III, 85–86). In one respect, Hobbes developed his notion a step further than in *The Elements of Law*. In discussing our inclination to progress from one object to another, Hobbes introduced the distinction between the "procuring" of objects of desire and the "assuring" of a contented life ("the power and means to live well"). Unlike mere "procuring," the aim of "assuring" is not "to enjoy once only, and for one instant of time; but, to assure for ever, the way of his future desire" (EW, III, 85). Thus, even a King "whose power is greatest" is nevertheless impelled to ever new conquests and triumphs. In effect, Hobbes is now saying that men's desires for power are without limit.

Acceptance of this viewpoint depends upon the recognition that man is oriented toward the future, not the present. Such an emphasis upon future goods led Hobbes to introduce another element into his equation — anxiety. Because of its position in a section concerning the origin of religion in chapter twelve, it has generally been overlooked in modern commentaries on Hobbes's theory of human nature. Anxiety is quite different from the more familiar fear of death — it arises from the paradox that "man observeth how one event hath been produced by another; and remembreth in them antecedence and consequence," yet "cannot assure himself of the true causes of things, (for the causes of good and evil fortune for the most part are invisible)" (EW, III, 94). It is thus "impossible for a man, who continually endeavoureth to secure himself against the evil he fears, and procure the good he desireth, not to be in a perpetual solicitude of the time to come" (EW, III, 95). The analysis comes to rest ultimately upon a brilliant comparison of "the estate" of "every man, especially those that are over provident" with that of Prometheus bound: "For as Prometheus, which interpreted, is, *the prudent man,* was bound to the hill Caucasus, a place of large prospect, where, an eagle feeding on his liver, devoured in the day, as much as was repaired in the night: so that man, which looks too far before him, in the care of future time, hath his heart all the day long, gnawed on by fear of death, poverty, or other calamity; and has no repose, nor pause of his anxiety, but in sleep" (EW, III, 95).

In chapter thirteen, Hobbes deals with man outside society. His approach undergoes one important development — a change more apparent than real. In place of the possibly abstruse "state of nature," Hobbes substitutes the simpler term "natural condition of mankind." In other respects, Hobbes's changes are mainly in the direction of greater clarity and vividness. The causes of contention are organized into three distinct categories: "competition" (the desire of equals to enjoy the same thing), "diffidence" (the right of any man, fearing for his life, to secure himself by "anticipation"), and "glory" (the pleasure of some men "in contemplating their own power in acts of conquest, which they pursue farther than their security requires") (EW, III, 111–112). Thus formulated, the causes of war acquire the analytic clarity of parallelism and symmetry: "The first, maketh men invade for gain; the second, for safety; and the third, for reputation. The first use violence, to make themselves masters of other mens persons, wives, children, and cattle; the second, to defend them; the third, for trifles, as a word, a smile, a different opinion, and any other signs of undervalue, either direct in their persons, or by reflexion in their kindred, their friends, their nation, their profession, or their name" (EW, III, 112).

Conscious as he is of the new concept of nature that he proposes and of its assertion that life without a common power to overawe us all differs widely from life in civil society, Hobbes's primary purpose in this chapter is to show that contention can be shown to arise from every kind of human behavior. To render his conception of such strife clear, Hobbes stresses that the natural condition of mankind includes not only "the act of fighting," but also the act of preparing to fight. As a result, Hobbes insists that "*time,* is to be considered in the nature of war; as it is in the nature of weather. For as the nature of foul weather, lieth not in a shower or two of rain; but in an inclination thereto of many days together, so the nature of war, consisteth not in actual fighting; but in the known disposition thereto, during all the time there is no assurance to the contrary" (EW, III, 113). A similar motive appears in Hobbes's elimination from *Leviathan* of his earlier view, embodied in both *the Elements of Law* and *De Cive,* that men can acquire and retain some private rights in nature. He now insists that "there be no propriety, no dominion, no *mine* and *thine* distinct." Since the security of these depends upon the protection of a common power, a man is assured only of what "he can get; and for so long, as he can keep it" (EW, III, 115).

To show the inherent instability of a time of war, Hobbes offers a vivid description of life in nature: "In such condition, there is no place for industry; because the fruit thereof is uncertain: and consequently no culture of the earth; no navigation, nor use of the commodities that may be imported by sea; no commodious building; no instruments of moving, and removing, such things as require much force; no knowledge of the face of the earth; no account of time; no arts; no letters; no society; and which is worst of all, continual fear, and danger of violent death; and the life of man, solitary, poor, nasty, brutish, and short" (EW, III, 113). Depicting the absolute solitude and stark barrenness of such conditions, Hobbes conveys a sense of life in which all activity, all motion has ceased. The use of parallelism and repetition removes any possibility of amelioration. This overpoweringly grave and serious description has, as Hobbes intended, immortalized his vision of man in nature. It is familiar to many who know little about Hobbes's philosophy apart from this passage.

One consequence of Hobbes's dramatic revision of his argument concerning the natural condition of mankind may have been his decision to abridge the account of man's natural rights in the beginning chapter fourteen, from five paragraphs in *De Cive* to two paragraphs in *Leviathan*. Hobbes's vision of the misery of man in nature expressed his conviction, more vividly than his earlier treatises had done, that the reverse of society is chaos. At the same time, he was evidently determined to avoid the impression that man is incapable of anything more than the ruthless pursuit of his own survival and advantage. Thus, the axiom that every man "by an impulsion of nature" desires his own good, no less than a stone moves downward, was dropped. As a result, it becomes impossible to confuse the declaration that every man has a "right" to defend himself with the axiom that "every man by natural necessity endeavours to defend his body" (EW, II, 17). The usage of "right" carries the connotation that we can somehow ignore it if we wish to.

To stress that the right of nature is "the liberty that each man hath, to use his own power, as he will himself, to the preservation of his own nature," Hobbes adds a separate paragraph on liberty as the absence of external impediments (EW, III, 116). At the same time, the statement in *De Cive* that "right is that which is not against reason" — which implied that a man may have a right to base his actions upon the natural passion of fear — is eliminated in favor of the position that man has the right to do any thing "which in his judgment and reason" shall enable him to preserve his nature. Then, to make his point clear, Hobbes restates it again: "RIGHT, consisteth in liberty to do, or to forbear; whereas LAW, determineth and bindeth to one of them; so that law, and right, differ as much as obligation, and liberty" (EW, III, 117).

What is the purpose of these changes? Since Hobbes did not explain himself, we can only speculate, but the emphasis upon liberty is surely suggestive. By defining "right" as the "liberty to do or forbear," Hobbes was evidently trying to pull himself free from the morass of natural necessity and to leave open the possibility of establishing social bonds between human beings. On the other hand, Hobbes also intended to make more emphatic his view that society is an artificial, not a natural phenomenon, and that its formation is a matter of choice, not necessity.[12] Perhaps the most significant aspect of Hobbes's political theory in *Leviathan* is his belief that all societies are problematic. For Hobbes, the social order is not an established, easily maintained equilibrium, but an order under continual threat of dissolution whose equilibrium is a never ending task. Hence he still insisted that "nature" — as distinguished from reason — dissociates and renders "men apt to invade and destroy one another" (EW, III, 113).

Just as Hobbes clarified his definition of right, so he also formulated the law of nature more emphatically in *Leviathan* than in *De*

*Cive.* In the earlier treatise, the fundamental law of nature is defined as "the dictate of right reason, conversant about those things which are either to be done or omitted for the constant preservation of life and members, as much as in us lies" (EW, II, 16). In *Leviathan,* it is stated as "a precept or general rule, found out by reason, by which a man is forbidden to do that, which is destructive of his life, or taketh away the means of preserving the same; and to omit that, by which he thinketh it may be best preserved." (EW, III, 116–117). By shifting from the plural to the singular and by introducing the notion of prohibition in the word "forbidden" Hobbes is able to state clearly that a law of nature is an obligation, which an individual can either obey or disobey. He also omits the phrase "right reason" with its potential for misinterpretation.

In chapters fourteen and fifteen of *Leviathan* Hobbes states nineteen laws of nature, one less than in *De Cive;* but while his list differs slightly from that of the earlier work, it remains basically unchanged. In chapter fifteen, however, Hobbes does introduce a new section in which he attempts to establish a firm basis for political obligation in the fundamental law of nature and so refute the insidious claims of the "fool" who whispers that there is no justice and therefore that a rebel's success constitutes its own justification. The argument of the fool is that, while "you may call" an act of treason or rebellion "unjust," "yet it can never be against reason, seeing all the voluntary actions of men tend to the benefit of themselves; and those actions are most reasonable, that conduce most to their own ends" (EW, III, 133).

Having thus posed the fool's argument in all its clarity and in terms that are uncomfortably close to his own, Hobbes then marshalled all of the resources of his logic to counter it. His theory of knowledge, as we have seen, denied that men can know the future with certainty. By this criteria, any reckless action whose consequences cannot be predicted is against reason: "when a man doth a thing, which notwithstanding any thing can be foreseen, and reckoned on, tendeth to his own destruction, however some accident which he could not expect, arriving may turn it to his benefit; yet such events do not make it reasonably or wisely done" (EW, III, 133). The effectiveness of this argument depends upon the distinction between a desire for present benefit in the narrow sense and for self-preservation in the broad sense. Only when this fundamental distinction is perceived, does Hobbes's reasoning acquire logical cogency.[13] Perhaps because he was aware that such an appeal is not enough to deter the resolute rebel from his undertaking,[14] Hobbes added a second argument in which he implied that rebellion cuts across both the third law of nature that covenants be performed and the tenth that no man take for himself what he is not content should be allowed for others. If a man refuses to adhere to these laws, then he renounces his right to the protection of the commonwealth, and others have the right to drive him out of society to perish by himself in nature (EW, III, 133–134).

Both of Hobbes's arguments illustrate the difficulty of constructing a theory that will persuade men, by reasons based upon a prudential rather than a transcendental foundation, that he ought to obey the law. Hobbes was of course as aware as later critics that such an argument was impossible to demonstrate with logical certitude, and as a result his appeal in this chapter seems directed not so much at the rebel as at others whose acceptance of the fool's "specious" reasoning makes the rebel's task much easier. Nevertheless, Hobbes was obviously disturbed by the fool's argument which, because of its seeming resemblance to his own views, constituted a threat to his system and its values. The uncompromising cynicism of the fool was a force, a subversive force, against which Hobbes had to struggle if he were to preserve the integrity and point of his political doctrine.

After completing his account of the laws of nature, Hobbes proceeds to introduce a chapter, "Of Persons and Personating," which has no corresponding chapter in *The Elements of Law* or in *De Cive*. This chapter replaces a chapter on "The Laws of Nature in Scripture." Hobbes's reason for dropping the latter may perhaps be found in his conviction, first expressed in the preceding chapter of *Leviathan,* that the laws of nature are rules which are not conducive to the attainment of "an eternal felicity after death," but only "to the preservation of man's life on earth." Although Hobbes opposed the former belief because it might tend to encourage rebellion against the temporal sovereign, his argument that "there is no natural knowledge of man's estate after death ... but only a belief grounded upon other men's sayings" (EW, III, 135), tends to render scriptural support for the laws of nature logically extraneous.

In his new sixteenth chapter, Hobbes apparently intended to remedy two deficiencies in his theory. First: Upon what basis can the actions of the sovereign be regarded as legitimate so that their results can be seen as binding? And second: In what sense can a multitude be said to be united in one person? In order to understand Hobbes's answer to these two questions, it is necessary to understand the sense in which the terms "person" and "persona" are used in this chapter. A "person" is he *"whose words or actions are considered, either as his own, or as presenting the words or actions of another man, or of any other thing, to whom they are attributed, whether truly or by fiction"* (EW, III, 147). In this sense, a man's "artificial" person as a magistrate or sovereign is inseparable from his individual existence as a "natural" person. A sovereign is one thing in respect to himself; another in respect to his responsibilities as representative of the actions and words of another. A "persona" signifies the *"disguise* or *outward appearance"* of a man, a meaning derived by Hobbes from the Greek and Roman theater where it was used to refer to the "mask" or "vizard" with which the actor covers his face. Thus an artificial person is the same as an actor, and "to *personate"* is "to *act*, or *represent* himself, or another; and he that acteth another, is said to bear his person, or act in his name" (EW, III, 148).

On the same principle, the person on whose behalf an actor performs is the "author" of his actions, in which case the "actor acteth by his authority." Since to authorize an action means to confer "a right to any act," it follows that when a sovereign acts "by authority" of a subject, he binds the subject or "author" to his actions, no less than if the subject had performed them himself. Of greater importance, the sovereign binds the subject to all the good or bad consequences of these actions. In Hobbes's opinion, it is only by the concentration of authority in the person of the sovereign that the evil of anarchy can be avoided. Furthermore, this view of the matter enables Hobbes to avoid, in part, the ambiguity that arose from his earlier insistence that in the commonwealth the multitude is united in one person. Now he insists that when he uses that phrase, he does not refer to "the *unity* of the represented," but to "the *unity* of the representer" (EW, III, 151), that is of the artificial person to whom the multitude transfers its rights. As a result, he is able to argue that a plurality, not unanimity, is sufficient to "be considered as the voice of them all." The covenant, therefore, can now be made without the unanimous consent of every man with every man — all that is needed is an agreement of all men to abide by the results of the majority.

## II    *"Of Commonwealth"*

In *Leviathan,* the final version of Hobbes's political thought embodied in part two, "Of Commonwealth," contains major revisions of parallel sections in earlier works: *De Corpore Politico* in *The Elements of Law* and "Of Dominion" in *De Cive.* The chapter comparing the three forms of government according to their respective inconveniences, for example, was dropped. An important new chapter, entitled "Of the Liberty of Subjects," was added. Chapters on the rights of lords over servants, of parents over children, and of places in scripture concerning the rights of government were combined into one chapter, "Of Dominion Paternal" (*Lev.,* II, 20). Conversely a single chapter concerning laws and trespasses (EL, II, 10; DeC, II, 14) was broken up and expanded into three separate chapters (*Lev.,* II, 26–28). Moreover, within part two we can find two groups of chapters which form internal units. The first, extending from chapter twenty-one to chapter twenty-five, develops the analogy contained in the title, of the state to a natural body. In the second unit, comprising chapters twenty-six through twenty-eight, Hobbes develops his theory of civil obligation and punishment.

In these chapters the major alterations appear in arguments that Hobbes obviously regarded not as logically demonstrated but only probably shown. There is one substantial revision, however, of Hobbes's central doctrine in *Leviathan.* It occurs in chapter eighteen, "Of the rights of the sovereign by institution." These rights are a logical deduction from earlier postulates that explain why a sovereign power must be obeyed. Hobbes's aim in this section was to find principles that were logical and compelling. Without a legitimate reason for obedience, human society reveals "that dissolute condition of masterless men, without subjection to laws, and a coercive power to tie their hands from rapine and revenge" (EW, III, 170). In *The Elements of Law* and *De Cive,* the rights of the sovereign had been derived from the consent of the multitude who transfer their rights to a chosen governor from fear of one another. Since this consent must be unanimous, it becomes extremely difficult for subjects of a sovereign to change the form of government or to repudiate the authority of the sovereign. Nonetheless, it does remain a possibility. In *Leviathan* Hobbes seeks to remove this possibility by developing the implications of his theory of representation set forth in chapter sixteen. Sovereignty, he now argues, is inalienable and cannot be conferred conditionally. Hence "they that are subjects ... cannot without his leave cast off monarchy, and return to the confusion of a disunited multitude" (EW, III, 160). For example, men cannot legitimately enter into a covenant with God that might conflict with political covenants. A covenant with God cannot be made "but by mediation of somebody that representeth God's person; which none doth but God's lieutenant, who hath sovereignty under God" (EW, III, 160–161). Hobbes's insistence here that the sovereign is God's lieutenant enables him to emphasize that the primary obligation of the sovereign is not to his subjects but to God. Hence it follows, in Hobbes's revision in *Leviathan,* that the sovereign is not himself a party to the covenant. Hobbes makes this point explicit: "because the right of bearing the person of them all, is given to him they make sovereign, by covenant only of one to another, and not of him to any of them; there can happen no breach of covenant on the part of the sovereign; and consequently none of his subjects, by any pretence of forfeiture, can be freed from his subjection" (EW, III, 161). Even if it were possible for a subject to perceive a breach of covenant by the sovereign, Hobbes adds that there could be no judge to decide the controversy and it would return "to the sword again" (EW, III, 161).

In thus defining political obligation, Hobbes's aim was not to describe the actual formation of civil governments, but to find reasons that could make obedience legitimate. It might easily be objected, however, that the reasons which Hobbes supplied, while logically consistent, provided the basis for a purely formal account of political obligation. Such an account was possibly hollow because it provided no emotional grounds for obedience. But Hobbes's political theory, as we have seen, is supported always by his knowing eye for man's various psychological inclinations. An awareness of the danger of disorder at the moment when society is on the verge of dissolution is an essential element of Hobbes's psychology.[15] As Hobbes describes it, this awareness is not so much a fear of organized conflict as a fear of plunder and fire, the peril of losing one's life and possessions, the dread of the pillage, arson, and violence unleashed by a brutal soldiery. Covenant whether by institution or acquisition initiates a political strategy by which these fearful tendencies are diverted from internal conflict to a united defense against external enemies. This strategy is Hobbes's central political myth. It may well be oblivious to other forms of disorder, but it does offer powerful emotional incentives for obedience.

To make his conception of the commonwealth as a real union of men rather than a mere multitude more comprehensible to the reader, Hobbes fashioned a new, more potent political symbol in *Leviathan*. Whereas in *De Cive* he had employed the classical terminology of the *civitas* or city to appeal to the intellect, he now relied upon scriptural allusions with a vastly stronger emotional appeal. The former symbol is obviously an outgrowth of Hobbes's conviction that civil society is not organic, — it has not been born of dependencies that can only be found in communities bound together by common traditions and experiences. In *De Cive,* the city is an artifact, the product of human reason and the outgrowth of a covenant among men. In such a contractual society, the motive for obedience is not to be found in the emotional ties of loyalty but in a rational conception of the need for peace and security.

It seems apparent that Hobbes's change in terminology in *Leviathan* is consciously designed to overcome the limitations inherent in such a dispassionately rational argument. While the logic of *Leviathan* is in no way incompatible with the political symbol of the city developed in *De Cive,* its rhetorical aim is very different: instead of appealing to reason alone, it attempts to reach man's passions and intellect simultaneously. In chapter seventeen, Hobbes proposes consideration of "that *mortal god,* to which we owe under the *immortal God,* our peace and defense" (EW, III, 158), as an inducement to reverence.[16] By contrast, in *De Cive* the conception of the city is presented in order to remove a philosophical difficulty that would, if allowed to remain, stifle impulses to obedience, and encourage each man to follow his own private conscience. There is a very great emotional difference between that which moves us to awe and that which merely prohibits us logically from disobedience.

In chapter eighteen, Hobbes is even more explicit: "As in the presence of the master, the servants are equal, and without any honour at all; so are the subjects, in the presence of the sovereign. And though they shine some more, some less, when they are out of his sight; yet in his presence, they shine no more than the stars in the presence of the sun'' (EW, III, 169). Here Hobbes not only stresses the emotional distance between sovereign and subject more emphatically than in the earlier treatises, but he obliquely calls attention to the implications of this change in emphasis. By employing the conventional metaphor of royalist panegyric, Hobbes reminds us that the authority of the sovereign is derived in his argument from the same source as in divine right theory. In Hobbes's view, there was clearly some common ground between two theories that differed widely but were not mutually exclusive.

The symbolism of the famous frontispiece of *Leviathan,* which is elaborated in part two of the work, is itself a product of Hobbes's rhetorical intention. The gigantic figure looming over the landscape, the arms and chest composed of innumerable persons, the sword, crown, and mitre, represent many arguments which are too complex and exact to be easily apprehended at once. They must rather be grasped imaginatively. For Hobbes, these figures symbolize the ''real unity'' of the people beyond faction and multitude, and the majesty of the office beyond the natural limitations of the person who holds it. Implicit in *Leviathan* is the belief that no commonwealth can arrive at a consciousness of its total unity without such symbols.

In order to amplify these symbols, Hobbes introduces a notion fundamentally at odds with the conception of the state as an artifact — that of an organic body. In the new chapters, twenty-two through twenty-four, Hobbes compares political ''systems'' to the ''muscles of a body natural'' (EW, III, 210), the public ministers to ''the parts organical'' (EW, III, 226), the *''plenty* and *distribution* of *materials''* to the nutrition conducing to the life of an organic body (EW, III, 232). In chapter twenty-nine, on the internal diseases of the commonwealth, Hobbes refers to ''the insatiable appetite, or *Bulimia,* of enlarging dominion; with the incurable *wounds* thereby many times received from the enemy'' (EW, III, 321). Another compares the doctrine of tyrannicide to the venom of ''a mad dog, which is a disease the physicians call *hydrophobia,* or *fear of water''* (EW, III, 315). Though somewhat labored, these analogies reveal the extent to which Hobbes sought to apply the analogy of an organism to civil government.

A concept of government measured in terms of an organic body was hardly a novelty to political theory. It had been a staple of philosophical discussion at least from the Middle Ages. The unique position of *Leviathan* in this tradition derives from its recognition that a political theory built on the principle of a social covenant demands a use of the organic analogy different from the prevailing one. Hobbes recognized that even a traditional analogy can be seen from a different perspective. In *Leviathan* his emphasis is on the union of elements, natural and artificial. Both are necessary, because man is both "matter" and "maker," creature and creator, a union of vitality and reason. Thus a government can never be purely contrived and rational; it must include emotional and vital as well as logical elements. Basic to Hobbes's unusual use of this analogy is the perception that every government is both organism and artifact.

## III   *Concerning Religion*

A Norwich divine named Charles Robotham characterized Hobbes's *Leviathan* in 1673 as "Malmesburian Hydra, the enormous Leviathan, the gigantic dragon, the hideous monstrosity and British beast, the Propagator of execrable doctrines, the Promulgator of mad wisdom, the Herald and Pugilist of impious death, the Insipid Venerator of a Material God, the Renowned Fabricator, of a monocondyte Symbol, the Depraved Renewer of old heresies to the faith, the Nonsensical roguish vendor of falsifications, a strenuous hoer of weeds and producer of deceits."[17] Robotham's apocalyptic mythology undoubtedly presented *Leviathan* as many clerics in the late seventeenth century wished to see it. The attitude is exactly paralleled in many polemical renderings of Hobbesian ideas; the only alternative to Christian orthodoxy for a majority of clergymen in the seventeenth century was atheism and libertinism. Critics like Robotham were accurate in perceiving the unconventional character of Hobbes's theology but were incapable or unwilling to distinguish between infidelity and an untraditional theology. Even men of philosophical and scientific training, who were aware of greater subtleties in philosophical inquiry, were often incapable of seeing how far Hobbes's heterodoxy was from simple atheism.

Such views appeared even before the publication of *Leviathan*. Bishop Bramhall's attack upon Hobbes arose out of a controversy that occurred in 1645. In the same year, Robert Baillie objected to Hobbes's appointment as a tutor in mathematics to the Prince of Wales on the grounds of his supposed atheistical principles.[18] Notwithstanding such criticisms, however, Hobbes devoted increasing attention to religion in his later political works. It had occupied only a few chapters in *The Elements of Law,* but approximately one fourth of *De Cive,* as we have seen, was concerned with religion. A full systematic exposition of Hobbes's philosophy of religion appeared in 1651 as the last two parts of *Leviathan;* together, they occupy as much bulk as the first two parts. Part three, entitled "Of a Christian Commonwealth," provides significant expansions of Hobbes's views in part three, "Of Religion," in *De Cive.* On the other hand, part four, "Of the Kingdom of Darkness," is from a different mold. A strange and often charming melange of Hobbes's views on demonology, witchcraft, exorcism, it provides a view of the philosopher as a religious controversialist, attempting to refute the doctrines of the church of Rome.

The basic elements of Hobbes's theology, however, are set forth in chapter thirty one of part two, "Of the Kingdom of God by Nature." Two important and interrelated themes emerge from this chapter. First, Hobbes regards the existence of God as rationally demonstrable. On the other hand, he also views the attributes of God as incomprehensible. The first theme rests upon a conventional version of the causal argument, first stated in *The Elements of Law.* God is the first link in the chain of causes: "by God, is understood the cause of the world" (EW, III, 351). For the second theme Hobbes makes use of a theory of knowledge that he regards as self-evident: insofar as an idea has content or represents objects, it must be finite. Much earlier in *Leviathan,* these two themes appear together in one sentence: "by the visible things of this world, and their admirable order, a man may conceive there is a cause of them, which men call God; and yet not have an idea, or image of him in his mind" (EW, III, 93). This combination of themes can be shown to be traditional.[19] It also conforms to the assumption of Galileo that an axiom can be logically demonstrated, even if it can never be empirically verified or perceived — for example, that a body in motion will continue in a straight line forever unless something else stops it.

The importance of this theology for Hobbes's erastianism can easily be shown. If a finite mind cannot have an adequate idea of God, it cannot know God's Word unless that Word is revealed directly to it. This conception does not mean that the term "God" has no meaning for Hobbes or that God's Word is inconceivable.

When God's Word does not differ from the laws of nature, it is known to all men; but when God does not reveal his Word directly to someone, that person need not obey it except by the authority of the sovereign power (EW, III, 378).

This argument lies at the heart of Hobbes's subordination of church and private spirit to the state in *Leviathan*. As we have seen, in *De Cive* Hobbes ascribed dominion in both spiritual and temporal matters to the civil sovereign. In *Leviathan,* Hobbes sought to purify religion of all mysterious and supernatural elements that would conflict with this position. In chapter thirty-two, the epistemological validity of dreams and visions is called into question; in chapter thirty-three, the authority of scripture is undermined; in chapter thirty-four, the notion of angels and spirits is supplanted by the doctrine of corporeality; in chapter thirty-five, the kingdom of God revealed in scripture is described as a civil kingdom; in chapter thirty-six, the scope of prophecy is limited; and in chapter thirty-seven, the potentiality for abuse in miracles is emphasized. In all of these chapters, Hobbes's purpose is not to destroy revealed Christianity, but to provide a theoretical foundation for his subordination of church and conscience to the state. It is evident, however, that he did not fully perceive the magnitude of the epistemological difficulties lurking beneath the surface of this enterprise, difficulties which remained unsuspected until the eighteenth century.

The fragility of the religious edifice that Hobbes sought to erect in part three of *Leviathan* is brought out by several considerations. In chapter thirty-two, "Of the Principles of Christian Politics," Hobbes examines the grounds for believing the alleged claims of individuals to have experienced visions, revelations, dreams, or prophecies. Hobbes is careful to admit that some visions are immune to doubt — those which are given to "a man immediately may be understood by those well enough, to whom he hath spoken" (EW, III, 361). However, a way is found to cast doubt on even the most evident visions. The argument that dreams are natural and often deceptive is used by Hobbes to show the untrustworthiness of private revelation: "to say he [God] hath spoken to him in a dream, is no more than to say he dreamed God spake to him" (EW, III, 361). But are there not some dreams and visions that cannot be shaken, even by this consideration? The possibility that men might be dreaming is to Hobbes insufficient in itself to lead us to doubt the validity of all supernatural voices. But he goes on to present another consideration that casts doubt on all forms of extraordinary inspiration: "though God Almighty can speak to a man by dreams, visions, voice and inspiration; yet he obliges no man to believe he hath so done to him that pretends it; who, being a man may err, and, which is more, may lie" (EW, III, 362). Hobbes's use of these considerations was limited to removing what he considered to be one of the most dangerous threats to the authority of the civil commonwealth: false prophecies (EW, III, 378–379). Later, however, similar considerations would be incorporated by the deists into a much more radical criticism of revealed Christianity.

Another example of the way in which Hobbes's skepticism acts to undermine the religious edifice of *Leviathan* occurs in his treatment of scripture in chapter thirty-three. Hobbes holds in *Leviathan* as in earlier works the conviction that the "only article of faith, which the Scripture maketh simply necessary to salvation, is this, that JESUS IS THE CHRIST" (EW, III, 590). Moreover, Hobbes expresses the personal belief in chapter thirty-three that "the Old, and New Testament, as we have them now, are the true registers of those things, which were done and said by the prophets, and apostles" (EW, III, 376). Yet, the possibility that any witness may err or lie is sufficient to catch in the net of doubt the testimony, not only of visionaries and fanatics but also of prophets and observers including the "writers of the New Testament."

We might well wonder why Hobbes makes use of such extreme criteria in building up the case against supernatural inspiration. Clearly, the argument that man has no way of proving that his dreams are not of natural origin can render suspect those revelations contained in scripture, as well as those which are given immediately. As Hobbes puts it in his discussion of prophecies in chapter thirty-six: "generally the prophets extraordinary in the Old Testament took notice of the word of God no otherwise, than from their dreams, or visions; that is to say, from the imaginations which they had in their sleep, or in an extasy: which imaginations in every true prophet were supernatural; but in false prophets were either natural or feigned" (EW, III, 418). The authority of scriptures apart, have we any way of telling which prophecies are supernatural and which are natural? Hobbes himself warns of our need to distinguish "between natural, and supernatural gifts" (EW, III, 423). The possibility of error is of course particularly disturbing, for

Hobbes's notion of what is necessary for salvation rests solely on the authority of scriptures.[20]

What preserves Hobbes's philosophy of religion from the implications of his radical skepticism concerning the validity of supernatural revelation is natural reason — the laws of nature "written in man's heart." Again and again, natural reason is invoked as a buttress for the authority of scripture and biblical revelation. In chapter thirty-three, he declares: "as far as they [scripture] differ not from the laws of nature, there is no doubt, but they are the law of God, and carry their authority with them, legible to all men that have the use of natural reason; but this is no other authority, then that of all other moral doctrine consonant to reason; the dictates whereof are laws, not *made*, but *eternal*" (EW, III, 378). Hobbes also insists in chapter thirty-six with regard to prophecy that "every man then was, and now is bound to make use of his natural reason, to apply to all prophecy those rules which God hath given us, to discern the true from the false" (EW, III, 425). Similar statements can be found in Hobbes's discussion of inspiration in chapters thirty-two and thirty-four and of miracles in chapter thirty-seven.

But this centrally important conclusion immediately presents a problem. If natural reason affords the means by which the validity of biblical revelation and scripture is tested, may it not also provide the means by which the conduct of the civil sovereign can be judged? Hobbes is aware of this difficulty and tries to resolve it through an appeal to another consideration — the fallibility of human judgments and human reason. Admitting in chapter forty-three that even "Christian Kings may err," Hobbes asks "but who shall judge? Shall a private man judge, when the question is of his own obedience? Or shall any man judge but he that is appointed thereto by the Church, that is, by the civil sovereign that representeth it? Or if the pope, or an apostle judge, may he not err in deducing of a consequence? Did not one of the two, St. Peter, or St. Paul err in a superstructure, when St. Paul withstood St. Peter to his face? There can therefore be no contradiction between the laws of God and the laws of a Christian commonwealth" (EW, III, 601). Hobbes's position here then becomes vulnerable to the charge that natural reason does not obviously possess the total immunity from error implied in the earlier chapters on prophecies, miracles, and supernatural visions.

In general, Hobbes's use of natural reason and divine omniscience to bridge the epistemological gaps between fallible and certain knowledge, between subjective delusion and divine revelation, was regarded as a *tour de force* by his contemporaries and immediate successors. Most of Hobbes's seventeenth century opponents simply ignored his arguments based upon reason and natural law, regarding them as gratuitous or as a sop to orthodoxy. These critics found it easy to cut through what they regarded as the protective screen of Hobbes's orthodoxy to perceive the hydra-headed monster of atheism lurking behind it.

Was Hobbes hypocritical? Was he afraid to advance his true beliefs? He certainly went to great pains to distinguish between a man's private beliefs and his public conformity to the established church. Such an attitude undoubtedly prompted Professor Leo Strauss to suggest that "many present-day scholars . . . do not seem to have a sufficient notion of the degree of circumspection or of accommodation to the accepted views that was required, in former ages, of 'deviationists'."[21] Hobbes must indeed have been aware of the accommodation required of such deviationists as Galileo, Borelli, and Descartes. When he was later confronted with the charge of heresy, he did indeed commit some manuscripts to the flames. Yet, it is difficult to accept this thesis when we recall that Hobbes, unlike Isaac Newton, was unwilling to submit, remain silent, or gloss over differences in matters of theology. For all his scorn of controversy and dogmatism, his own combative temperament can still be glimpsed in his own dogmatism, in the boldness of his formulations, and especially in the unremitting stubbornness with which he persisted in advancing heterodox arguments in the face of certain public hostility.

The variety, density, and complexity of the third book of *Leviathan* are the results of Hobbes's unwillingness to accommodate himself to received opinion. Throughout the third book, he conducts two different lines of investigation which are never harmonized into a balanced, unified philosophy of religion. From chapters thirty-two through thirty-seven, Hobbes develops a critical attitude toward the belief that men can be supernaturally inspired which is supported by the principle that individuals err and may even lie. This principle as we have seen is the basis of Hobbes skepticism and is relentlessly applied to miracles, prophecies, visions, and all forms of indirect evidence for revelation including even biblical witnesses.

In contrast to his skeptical movement, Hobbes indulges his interest in religious issues in the later chapters of part three and employs the characteristic method of religious controversialists, the dogmatic examination of biblical texts. In chapter thirty-eight, the traditional conception of eternal damnation is rejected; in chapter thirty-nine — which is based upon chapter seventeen, sections nineteen through twenty-two, of *De Cive* — the word church is redefined to mean a Christian commonwealth; in chapters forty and forty-one, which parallel chapters sixteen and seventeen of *De Cive,* scriptural support is adduced for Hobbes's erastianism; in chapter forty-two, the trinity is held to refer to Moses, the Apostles, and Christ; and in chapter forty-three, which corresponds to the last chapter of *De Cive,* Hobbes sets forth what he believes are the requirements necessary for salvation. Perhaps nothing that Hobbes wrote offers stronger evidence of his independence than these chapters. But it is not always apparent that his lengthy, subtle, abstruse investigations of scriptural texts are germane to Hobbes's laying a solid foundation for the subordination of church to state. Nor does his critical attack upon certain orthodox doctrines appear any more relevant to that end.

The unity of Hobbes's religious thought is perhaps most evident in the way he apprehends the kingdom of God. So compelling was the ideal of the civil commonwealth to Hobbes that he even transposed it from the secular to the religious sphere: "Lastly, seeing it hath been already proved out of divers evident places of Scripture, in chap. xxxv of this book, that the kingdom of God is a civil commonwealth, where God himself is sovereign, by virtue first of the *old,* and since of the *new* covenant, wherein he reigneth by his vicar or lieutenant; the same places do therefore also prove, that after the coming again of our Saviour in his majesty and glory, to reign actually and eternally, the Kingdom of God is to be on earth" (EW, III, 444). The phrases, "God the King," and "Christ the King," which recur many times in the third part of *Leviathan,* suggest that God is an absolute monarch, that worshippers have a personal relationship to a king, not to abstract attributes, and that after the resurrection, Christ will govern in triumph over the elect in an ideal commonwealth on earth. It is not surprising therefore that Hobbes occasionally gives expression in this part of *Leviathan* to a theology of glory in stately rhetoric. Nowhere is there a doubt concerning the majesty of God. On the contrary, there appears to be genuine, if restrained, awe at the power and majesty of the divine king: "Of the world to come, St. Peter speaks (2 *Pet. iii* 13) *Nevertheless we according to his promise look for new heavens, and a new earth.* This is that WORLD, wherein Christ coming down from heaven in the clouds, with great power, and glory, shall send his angels, and shall gather together his elect, from the four winds, and from the uttermost parts of the earth, and thenceforth reign over them, under his Father, everlastingly" (EW, III, 456). In such passages, Hobbes successfully communicates his sense of the almost corporeal existence of an invisible God and his awed acquiescence before His power. His deity is a God of majesty and power, and this may help to explain why Hobbes, who had developed a radical skepticism concerning the validity of religious testimony, should have succumbed to the spell of the Book of Job. Nothing could better illustrate the particular character of Hobbes's religious faith and its close relationship to his political thought.

## CHAPTER 6

# Hobbes and Critical Theory

BECAUSE of Hobbes's acumen as a thinker, his views on poetry have an uncommon significance. Though not primarily interested in literary criticism and limited by the critical principles of his own time, Hobbes made incisive and often far-reaching observations about the nature of poetry, the literary genres, and the creative process. As we might expect, his critical writings are occasional and fragmentary. Besides the preface to his translation of Thucydides, they consist of *The Answer to Sir William Davenant's Preface before Gondibert,* the letter to Edward Howard reprinted as preface to Howard's epic poem *The British Princess* (1669), and the preface to Hobbes's translation of Homer's *Iliad* and *Odyssey,* published when he was seventy-seven years old, as well as important passages in *The Elements of Law, De Cive,* and *Leviathan.*

In spite of the absence of any systematic design in these discussions, they often seem to reflect the preoccupations of Hobbes's major philosophical works, especially his nominalism, skepticism, and empiricism. At the same time, however, they offer convincing proof that Hobbes's humanism survived his conversion from history to philosophy. This humanism is particularly evident, not only in the studied gracefulness of his critical prefaces, but also in their content. Hobbes still affirms in 1650, for example, that the end of poetry is "to adorn virtue, and procure her lovers" (EW, IV, 447). We should not put too much emphasis upon this comment, but it does seem to imply the existence of virtue as an objective entity, which can be perceived, if not directly, then at least through the medium of poetic fable. Hobbes's humanism is equally apparent in his lasting interest in the heroic poem, an interest manifested not only in his prefaces to two of the most ambitious attempts at epic poetry in the 1650's and 1660's but also in his own translation of Homer's *Iliad* and *Odyssey.* These interests are not irrelevant to the traditional humanism which, as we have seen, permeates the preface and dedication to the translation of Thucydides.

### I  The Answer of Mr. Hobbes to Sir William Davenant's Preface before Gondibert

During his stay in Paris, Hobbes belonged to a literary circle of which we know little, except that it included Sir William Davenant, Abraham Cowley, Edmund Waller and other exiled royalist poets. Hobbes's conversations with Davenant may have stimulated his own reflections about the nature of poetry and the poetic process. The result, *The Answer to the Preface before Gondibert,* was published in 1650, together with Davenant's letter, as a preface to Davenant's unfinished heroic poem, *Gondibert.* It contains, along with Hobbes's sympathetic praise of Davenant's epic, his fullest discussion of poetry.

Hobbes does not appear to have been guided in this essay, as he was in his philosophical works, by any rigorous philosophical or "scientific" method; his approach is rather distinguished by its informality and gracefulness, reflecting, perhaps, the influence of Michel Eyquem de Montaigne. However unsystematic his approach may appear, a systematic structure of ideas can be discerned in Hobbes's *Answer to Davenant's Preface.*

### 1.  *Hobbes's conception of poetry*

Central to Hobbes's critical doctrine is his conception of poetry. Like all heirs to the classical tradition of Aristotle, Horace, and Quintilian, Hobbes sees poetry as a form of discourse, having its own specific ends as well as the means to achieve those ends. But Hobbes goes much further than many seventeenth century critics in emphasizing the qualitative and quantitative differences between poetry and other forms of discourse. In contrast to Sir Philip Sidney, for instance, Hobbes defines poetry in such a way as to make verse an essential attribute. Prose, by and large, he treats as a shapeless medium, "the ways and motions" of which are "uncertain and undistinguished, like the way and motion of a ship in the sea" (EW, IV, 446). The competition between them is decidedly unequal: "if prose contend with verse, it is often with disadvantage and, as it were, on foot against the strength and wings of Pegasus" (EW, IV, 445). In a statement amazing for one who became a master of English prose, Hobbes declares that its effects are likely "not only to discompose the best composers, but also to disappoint sometimes the most attentive reader, and put him to hunt counter for the sense'' (EW, IV, 446).

Hobbes stops short, however, of the view of naïve critics who ''take poesie for whatsoever is writ in verse.'' He introduces two additional criteria by which poetry must be defined — choice of subject and imitation. The first serves to differentiate the poet from the philosopher (''the subject of a poem is the manners of men, not natural causes''); this neat distinction allows Hobbes to exclude from the ranks of poets ''Empedocles and Lucretius, natural philosophers'' and from poetry and the ''moral precepts of Phoclylides, Theognis, and the quatrains of Pybrach'' (EW, IV, 445). The second enables us to separate the poet from the historian: ''manners feigned, as the name of poesy imports, not found in men.'' Lucan, on this account, is given the title of historian rather than poet (EW, IV, 455).

With his conception of ''truth'' as an integral part of history, it is fitting that when Hobbes considers imitation at greater length, ''truth'' retains its importance. Hobbes insists that in one respect truth is as much the aim of the poet as of the historian: ''for as truth is the bound of historical, so the resemblance of truth is the utmost limit of poetical liberty. In old time amongst the heathen, such strange fictions and metamorphoses were not so remote from the articles of their faith, as they are now from ours, and therefore were not so unpleasant. Beyond the actual works of nature a poet may now go; but beyond the conceived possibility of nature, never'' (EW, IV, 451–452). Hobbes clearly suggests that the situations, actions, and characters, portrayed or evoked, must strike us as true to life. Fantasy and poetic mythology are excluded, though the phrase ''conceived possibility of nature'' surely allows for the existence of utopian works. Even so, however, we must still feel these works to be true to something in nature: this feeling is lost in the ''strange fictions and metamorphoses'' of the heathens. Nonetheless, by using the term ''resemblance of truth'' — which also implies the existence of differences — Hobbes avoids the narrow interpretation of poetry as a mere likeness or copy.

## 2.  The Literary Genres

Hobbes had said that the philosopher should attempt to discover the truth through reasoning rather than trust in ''the authority of books." Rather similarly, he insists that the poet must borrow from his own "experience and knowledge of nature, specially human nature," rather than from books — the "ordinary boxes of counterfeit complexion" (EW, IV, 452–453). This bias obviously leaves no room for the conventional theory of rhetorical imitation. It also serves to explain Hobbes's revision of the traditional classi-fication of poetic kinds. For Hobbes, the major genres of poetry — *"heroic, scommatick,* and *pastoral"* — correspond to the major "regions of mankind, *court, city* and *country"* (EW, IV, 443). Dif-ferences in the manner of representation "which sometimes is *narrative . . .* sometimes *dramatic"* account for a further division of the heroic into epic poem and tragedy, the scommatic into satire and comedy, and pastoral into bucolic and pastoral comedy. By these distinctions, Hobbes alters dramatically the classical and Renaissance theory of genres. In place of differences based upon the study of approved models, he substitutes a simple classification based upon the poet's direct knowledge of immediate social reality. Sketchy as it is, this theory seems to foreshadow certain trends in Augustan poetry. The explicit association between the heroic poem and the court anticipates two important Augustan genres — the state panegyric and the historical poem. The connection between satire and the city looks forward to the essentially urban character of Restoration comedy and Augustan verse satire. Likewise, Hobbes's identification of pastoral with the actual countryside, rather than with Arcadia, seems to look toward the increasingly realistic concerns of such eighteenth-century pastoralists as John Gay, Oliver Goldsmith and George Crabbe. This classification obviously leaves little room for lyric poems, which are reduced in Hobbes's schema to "essays, and parts of an entire poem" (EW, IV, 444).

## 3. *Fancy and Judgment*

The originality of Hobbes's critical theory in *The Answer to Davenant's Preface* extends beyond his ideas about the literary genres. In this treatise Hobbes also examines the processes by which poetry comes into existence. The significance of this under-taking for the history of criticism can scarcely be overstated. What he offers is an enlargement of the traditional conception of the poet. From classical antiquity through the Renaissance, critical dis-cussion had focused upon the question of whether poets rely upon art or upon a mysterious force, poetic inspiration. The poetic process had not been important beyond its implicit presence in the notion of native genius, a notion which had never been defined. To explain how poems are brought into existence, Hobbes seized upon two psychological terms ready at hand, but also largely undefined. These were fancy and judgment. With Hobbes's explanation of these terms, the creative process begins to assume a consciously generalized formulation and to take on its later shape.

It is easy to underestimate Hobbes's achievement and to see in the prominence of judgment in his theory "a rationalistic distrust of the imagination."[1] Compared to later, Romantic explanations of the poetic process, his theory is undoubtedly weighted in favor of judgment. Yet the ambiguity of his emphasis, in the light of Hobbes's other writings, seems to require a more complicated explanation than a simple desire to undermine the imagination.

To understand Hobbes's basic approach to the poetic process, it is essential to remember that it springs from the same source as his approach to the human mind as a whole. We should recall that Hobbes's epistemology is shaped by a skepticism concerning the authenticity of alleged claims by individuals to have been divinely inspired, a skepticism most fully articulated in *Leviathan*. Translated into critical terms, what this skepticism meant — for Hobbes at least — was an insistence that the poet should be extremely cautious about presuming "to speak by inspiration, like a bagpipe" (EW, IV, 448). Hobbes uses the analogy of a "bagpipe" here to imply that when the poet presumes to "speak by inspiration," he gives up any claim to a special virtue for his contribution to poetry. In fact the poet who wishes to have his reader believe that he is inspired by the muses is generally prompted, in Hobbes's opinion, by no more than an uncritical commitment to an outmoded convention. Hobbes professes to find this commitment hard to understand: "why a Christian should think it an ornament to his poem, either to profane the true God, or invoke a false one, I can imagine no cause, but a reasonless imitation of custom" (EW, IV, 448).

This passage occurs in the paragraph immediately preceding Hobbes's analysis of fancy and judgment, and its position suggests that in formulating a psychology of poetic creation, Hobbes might have been consciously seeking an alternative to the view that poetry is divinely inspired. Because the fancy is akin to poetic inspiration in its independence of the will, it would be more suitable for this purpose than the judgment. As an alternative, the fancy would take the place of inspiration — not the fancy as constituted elsewhere in Hobbes's writings, limited and fallible, but the fancy as it could be conceived if it were preserved from error, and endowed with some of the same attributes as inspiration: energy, quickness, and spontaneity. Evidence to support this conclusion is provided by a consideration of the rather surprising change that takes place in the relations between fancy and judgment in the "Time and education" passage.

At the outset, Hobbes's passage in *The Answer to Davenant* defines the poetic process by resorting to a conventional distinction in which the judgment is assigned "the strength and structure" and fancy "the ornaments" of a poem. Unequal emphasis is placed upon the two terms; ornaments are little more than embellishments added to a pre-existing structure. By the end of the passage, however, the focus has shifted from judgment to fancy and a rather narrowly rhetorical conception of poetry is quietly supplanted by a much more flexible one for the purpose of offering the poet an alternative to the doctrine that poetry is divinely inspired.

Judgment is defined as a faculty which orders the materials of the memory, ascertaining their similarities, relations, or correspondences to the external world: "judgment, the severer sister, busieth her self in a grave and rigid examination of all the parts of nature, and in registering by letters, their order, causes, uses, differences and resemblances" (EW, IV, 449). The role of judgment is gradually altered from that proposed at the outset of Hobbes's passage. A "rigid examination of all the parts of nature" mainly concerns their selection and arrangement. By itself, such an examination cannot invent a subject or dispose of its parts in the most effective manner. For this process, the fancy is also required. The role of judgment is to provide the research in such a way that the fancy "when any work of art is to be performed, finds her materials at hand and prepared for use, and needs no more than a swift motion over them, that what she wants, and is there to be had, may not lie to long unespied."

Hobbes's use of judgment in this sense illustrates the importance of its position as the third in a sequence of stages in the poetical process. An explanation for its rather surprising position in this sequence — after memory, yet before the fancy — may be found in a distinction Hobbes makes in *De Corpore* between sensation and memory. In sensation, we are passively affected by the impact on us of bodies outside ourselves; hence sensations involve no explicit self-consciousness. By contrast, memory is almost a sixth sense consisting of comparisons between present and past images and of the perception of differences between them. It is by way of such comparisons that we order our thoughts. The completion of this process is defined by Hobbes in terms of the common meaning of the word "sense," that is "the judgment we make of objects by their phantasms; namely, by comparing and distinguishing those phantasms" (EW, I, 393). Judgment is thus wholly dependent upon the senses for its materials, and since nothing can be presented for comparison but by the memory, judgment is equally dependent upon memory.

If the judgment has already ascertained the mimetic value of its images, the fancy — freed from the danger of error present when it acts prior to judgment in the poetic process — can assume a vastly enlarged role in which it rivals the claim of poetic inspiration. Whereas fancy first simply referred to the application of pleasing similes, it now connects the activities of the poet to those of the philosopher:

whereby the fancy, when any work of art is to be performed, finds her materials at hand and prepared for use, and needs no more than a swift motion over them, that what she wants, and is there to be had, may not lie too long unespied. So that when she seemeth to fly from one Indies to the other, and from heaven to earth, and to penetrate into the hardest matter, and obscurest places, into the future, and into her self, and all this in a point of time, the voyage is not very great, her self being all she seeks. And her wonderful celerity, consisteth not so much in motion, as in copious imagery discreetly ordered, and perfectly registered in the memory; which most men under the name of philosophy have a glimpse of, and is pretended to by many, that grossly mistaking her, embrace contention in her place. (EW, IV, 449)

Here Hobbes transforms the psychic motion of the fancy, which is itself beyond the range of sense perception, into a perception of movement through space. Although its materials are derived from sense experience and ordered by judgment, the fancy appears in this transformation as an internalized image of Pegasus, the legendary embodiment of poetic inspiration. Its operation is perhaps best described as a vital, seemingly random motion which is clearly distinguished from mental activities of a practical order, on the one hand, and from those which are purely speculative on the other. The reference to "Indies" suggests the impractical aims of Hobbes's fancy. This Indies of the mind seems to hold forth promise of a rich cargo of images and fabulous events. It is only the "wonderful celerity" of the fancy that makes these treasures available to the mind, by contracting its motion into a single moment, as it were, a "point of time."

The metamorphosis of sense experience into "something rich and strange" through the operations of the fancy is the notion upon which the remainder of the passage works. It enables Hobbes to include within the "marvellous effects" of the fancy even the practical activities of the mind. *The Answer to Davenant* goes on to unfold a lofty conception of the fancy as the source not only of poetry, but of all the achievements of civilization, whether scientific or artistic. Hobbes's prose reveals a rare tendency toward extravagance when he speaks of the effects of the fancy's operations:

But so far forth as the fancy of man has traced the ways of true philosophy, so far it hath produced very marvellous effects to the benefit of mankind. All that is beautiful or defensible in building; or marvellous in engines and instruments of motion; whatsoever commodity men receive from the observation of the heavens, from the description of the earth, from the account of time, from walking on the seas; and whatsoever distinguiseth the civility of Europe, from the barbarity of the American savages; is the workmanship of fancy, but guided by the precepts of true philosophy. (EW, IV, 449–450)

We must certainly make some allowance for the unusual fervor of this passage. Hobbes customarily employs the word "fancy" as a synonym for what he means by "imagination," a passive faculty more acted upon than acting. And yet this passage is noteworthy, because it shows that Hobbes conceived of a faculty of mind never precisely defined before but which "performs" actively, both as the discoverer of raw materials and as the architect who builds with them. The notion of creativity inherent in these two functions has remained essential to subsequent developments in English critical thought.

## 4. *Fancy and Judgment in* The Elements of Law

Long before *The Answer to Davenant,* Hobbes had put forth in *The Elements of Law* a different but equally influential account of the fancy and judgment. However, the two explanations vary considerably in their assessment of the relative value of these terms. In *The Answer to Davenant,* Hobbes moves as we have seen from a view in which the fancy is subordinated to judgment to one which establishes the authority of the fancy as an independent faculty. In *The Elements of Law,* however, Hobbes's distinction implicitly affirms the preeminence of judgment in the creative process.

In *The Elements of Law* Hobbes at first seems to regard fancy and judgment as coordinate powers, two aspects of a single whole which he defines as wit:

The contrary hereunto, is that quick ranging of mind described chap. 4, sect. 3, which is joined with curiosity of comparing the things that come into his mind one with another. In which comparison, a man delighteth himself either with finding unexpected similitude in things, otherwise much unlike, in which men place the excellency of FANCY: and from thence proceed those grateful similies, metaphors, and other tropes, by which both poets and orators have it in their power to make things please or displease, and shew well or ill to others, as they like themselves; or else in discerning suddenly dissimilitude in things that otherwise appear the same. And this virtue of the mind is that by which men attain to exact and perfect knowledge: and the pleasure thereof consisteth in continual instruction, and in distinction of persons, places, and seasons; it is commonly termed by the name of JUDGMENT: for, to judge is nothing else, but to distinguish and discern; and both fancy and judgment are commonly comprehended under the name of WIT, which seemeth a tenuity and agility of spirits, contrary to that restiveness of the spirits supposed in those that are dull. (I. 10. 4)

As we might expect, Hobbes's terms are based upon the vocabularies of traditional philosophy and poetics, vocabularies already freighted with implications for the workings of the mind. Aristotle, to whom Hobbes often refers in his writings, stated in a well-known passage in *The Poetics* that "the ability to construct good metaphors implies the ability to see essential similarities.. Such an ability, he adds, "is not possible to obtain from another." Hence it is "in itself a sign of genius." (1459[a]11).[2] The import of this passage for Hobbes is that it treats metaphor as a mode of perception and not simply as a literary ornament. By insisting that the process of apprehending metaphors cannot be taught, Aristotle implies that such a process is not a mere literary technique but an act of mind. Hobbes reveals his debt to Aristotle by attaching this act of mind to a specific faculty — namely, fancy. Hobbes's conception of the process of judging evinces a similar pattern to Aristotle's idea of creating metaphor. In Hobbes's theory, there is the same use of a traditional notion with psychological implications — in this case of definition "per genus et differentiam (by class and differences)." There is the same adaptation of this term to a specific power of the mind. Just as "definition" is a twofold sequence in which we note the class to which something belongs, then add its *differentia,* so the activity of judgment consists of discovering differences in things apparently alike, thus presupposing them already organized by the mind into classes.

Hobbes's procedure then is to attach the traditional terminology of classical philosophy to specific powers of the mind: fancy is related to metaphor; judgment to definition. But by itself such a procedure does not account for the empirical bias in favor of judgment in Hobbes's definition. The answer is undoubtedly to be found in Hobbes's nominalism.

Although the view of judgment in seventeenth century criticism has sometimes been regarded as Neo-Platonic, it seems clear that as formulated by Hobbes in *The Elements of Law* (I., 10, 4) its affinity is rather with his nominalist theory of names. According to Hobbes, as we have seen, all things and all our images of things are individual; thus "there is nothing in the world universal but names." This notion is basic to an understanding of his distinction between fancy and judgment in *The Elements of Law.* As a faculty for discovering "unexpected similitude in things otherwise much unlike," the fancy presupposes their particularity. To discover resemblances between particular things therefore is to disregard what makes them unique. Insofar as such a process leads the poet to assume that things are actually ordered into kinds, it lays him open to the charge of verbal manipulations unrelated to their true nature. On the other hand, judgment is a power by which we discern "suddenly dissimilitude in things that otherwise appear the same." The key word in this sentence is "appear"; it is the only word in the entire passage that reveals the implicit superiority of judgment to fancy, Hobbes assumes that things are particular; in

treating judgment, he implies that they only appear to be constituted as classes. The implication of this distinction for poetry is
obvious. Judgment for Hobbes answers a concern to insist upon
the particularity of things and to preserve our apprehension of
them from any distortion by purely verbal constructions.

The implications for poetry inherent in this distinction become
clearer when we contrast the operations of the fancy with those of
the judgment. The fancy possesses a power to interpose a verbal
structure between the reader and the world. The interposition of
this structure gives us satisfaction, the satisfaction of "agreeable
Visions," but it also poses a danger: we can easily regard these
visions, not as creations in themselves, but as substitutes for external objects. When we perceive the real differences which point up
the nature of something, however, we gain the deeper, less immediate satisfaction of instruction. Since these differences are largely
conveyed through particulars, the distinction further implies that
there is a natural tendency to concreteness in the operations of
judgment. By thus incorporating a bias in favor of differences over
resemblances, this distinction may provide a partial explanation for
the predominantly empirical nature of English poetry during the
Restoration and eighteenth century. This view is corroborated by
the conclusions of Josephine Miles that the distinctive feature of
poets writing at the beginning of the eighteenth century was their
"abrupt abandoning of a conceptual vocabulary in favor of a sensory one."[3]

## II  *"To the Reader, Concerning the Virtues of the Heroic Poem'*

Hobbes again expounded his ideas about poetry in the brief and
general letter to Sir Edward Howard (1669), in which he almost
seems to anticipate the storm of ridicule which greeted Howard's
abortive attempt at the epic poem. A fuller exposition of Hobbes's
critical ideas appears in "To the Reader, Concerning the Virtues of
the Heroic Poem," published as a preface in 1679 to his translation
of Homer's *Iliad* and *Odyssey*. Although it bears a superficial
resemblance to *The Answer to Davenant*, Hobbes's essay concerning the virtues of the heroic poem is in fact markedly inferior to the
earlier work in originality and complexity. It reverts, for example,

from a psychological theory of poetic creation to an older conception of fancy and judgment as "virtues" of the poet.

Hobbes begins by asserting that the "design" of a heroic poem is "not only to profit, but also to delight the reader" (EW, X, iii). By profit, Hobbes does not mean an "accession of wealth either to the poet, or to the reader" but rather an "accession of prudence, justice, and fortitude, by the example of such great and noble persons as he introduceth speaking, or describeth acting." In contrast to his earlier views, Hobbes's pronouncements on the ethical function of poetry in the preface to Homer are brief and perfunctory. We may wonder what he actually thought by this time about the efficacy of this theory. Significantly, his answer reveals a considerable measure of pessimism: "all men love to behold, though not to practice virtue." Profit thus becomes in the final analysis almost negligible: "so that at last the work of an heroic poet is no more but to furnish an ingenuous reader, when his leisure abounds, with the diversion of an honest and delightful story, whether true or feigned" (EW, X, iii).

The problem of appealing to the ideal reader thus becomes a central preoccupation of Hobbes's preface. It is consonant with his aims as a translator, and it dictates the plan of the work — an enumeration of the "virtues" that "concur to make the reading of an heroic poem pleasant." The first part of the preface discusses these virtues in general terms, while the second parts repeats them for the purposes of comparing the relative merits of Homer, Virgil and Lucan, the only poets whom "for their excellency," says Hobbes, he has "read, or heard compared" (EW, X, vii).

In this context, Hobbes's emphasis upon diction and style at the expense of plot and character becomes comprehensible. The poet should try to please the reader, and to achieve this aim, Hobbes recommends a cultivation of "discretion," by which he means a strengthened sense of "propriety" and clarity. Thus "the first indiscretion" of the poet, according to Hobbes, is the use of words as "are not sufficiently known" (EW, X, iv). These include any terms beyond the comprehension of the ordinary reader—i.e., "foreign words," "the names of instruments and tools of artificers, and words of art." In a similar manner, Hobbes's treatment of style places a premium on the comfort and ease of the reader: "the order of words, when placed as they ought to be, carries a light before it, whereby a man may foresee the length of his period, as a torch in the night shows a man the stops and uneveness in his way. But when placed unnaturally, the reader will often find unexpected checks, and be forced to go back and hunt for the sense, and suffer such unease, as in a coach a man unexpectedly finds in passing over a furrow" (EW, X, iv–v).

A concern for the reader's preferences results in a devaluation of the fancy in the preface. A complex process is divorced from its original context, trivialized, and reduced to the status of a simple mechanism for giving the reader what he wants. Indeed, the fancy now owes its importance, not to its function, but to its popular reputation: "For men more generally affect and admire fancy than they do either judgment, or reason, or memory, or any other intellectual virtue, and for the pleasantness of it, give to it alone the name of wit, accounting reason and judgment but for a dull entertainment. For in fancy consisteth the sublimity of a poet, which is that poetical fury which the readers, for the most part, call for" (EW, X, v). This is a view of the fancy which is virtually indistinguishable from Locke's, as set forth in the *Essay Concerning Human Understanding*.

The Renaissance conception of the ethical function of poetry survives in an attenuated form in Hobbes's preface. What had originally been a deeply felt sense of the poet's mission is transformed into a concern for "decency" in description. It is most evident in Hobbes's insistence upon the poet's need to maintain "justice and impartiality." According to Hobbes, "as far as the truth of fact can defame a man, so far they are alllowed to blemish the reputation of persons. But to do the same upon report, or by inference, is below the dignity, not only of a hero, but of a man." Such a concern is certainly valid, but largely negative: it is not ennobling, nor does it reveal any truths of universal validity.

This preoccupation with factual rather than universal truth underlies the confusion between poetry and history in the preface. The chief difference between them is now exclusively formal: "a history is wholly related by the writer; but in an heroic poem the narration is, a great part of it, put upon some of the persons introduced by the poet" (EW, X, v). Even this distinction is blurred in Hobbes's concern for "the reputation of persons." The virtues he celebrates — justice and impartiality — are more suitable to the journalist and historian than to the poet. From this perspective, it is only a short step to the opinion that the Homeric epics are, except for "the introduction of their Gods ... so many histories in verse: where Homer has woven so many histories together as contain the whole learning of the time" (EW, X, vii).

Such is the content of Hobbes's last critical work. Although inferior in originality to his earlier writings on poetry, it is not without appeal. Not the least attractive merit of this preface is Hobbes's own lively enthusiasm, that personal note expressed most directly in his forceful, pungent wit. This enthusiasm accounts for the direct if sometimes provocative and irritating appeal which he can still make to us, even when his ideas have ceased to have any immediate interest.

CHAPTER 7

# The Legacy of Thomas Hobbes

BECAUSE the reaction of many of Hobbes's contemporaries to his ideas was so extreme, it has been difficult to assess the precise degree of his influence on such individual writers of the period as Dryden or Locke. There is no doubt that Hobbes's theories aroused a storm of nontroversy in England. John Bowles's survey of the reaction to his political thought attests to this. So also does Samuel I. Mintz's study of the objections of opponents to his metaphysics and moral philosophy.[2] In general these adversaries reflect the temper of the times, but this temper was by no means unanimous, and the philosopher who was condemned in many of the pulpits of London still had his partisans. There were also a considerable number of readers with sufficient discrimination to appreciate specific aspects of Hobbes's thought without endorsing his system as a whole. Quentin Skinner has shown that Hobbes's political theory was received favorably by a number of groups: "Hobbists," serious continental thinkers like Leibniz and Pufendorf, and the various proponents of a *de facto* theory of political obligation, who argued after both the English Civil War in 1650 and the Glorious Revolution in 1688 that obedience must be given to whatever government is in power.[3] To these groups, we may also add prominent literary figures: seventeenth century writers as diverse as Cowley, John Wilmot, Earl of Rochester, and Davenant registered the impact of Hobbesian ideas. In the early eighteenth century Bernard Mandeville and Daniel Defoe drew inspiration from Hobbes and helped to make his thought known indirectly to many readers.

## I  *Hobbism*

We cannot really understand Hobbes's influence on his contem-

146

poraries without first distinguishing "Hobbism" — an unstable amalgam of opinions ascribed to Hobbes by writers unsympathetic to his position — from Hobbes's own writings. The attitude of poets and dramatists toward Hobbes during the Restoration may have been based not so much on Hobbes's actual thought as on simplified versions of his ideas provided by such lively controversialists as John Eachard whose *Mr. Hobb's State of Nature Considered* went through four editions between 1672 and 1696. In their most exaggerated form, these ideas are transmuted into the ideology of evildoers in the drama of the period. The treatment of these figures faithfully follows the characterization of *Leviathan* as "a very bad book" by Archbishop Tillotson.[4] In George Farquhar's *The Constant Couple* (1699), for example, Vizard is represented reading what seems to be *The Practice of Piety* but is in fact *Leviathan*. Maskwell in William Congreve's *The Double Dealer* (1694) and Scandal in *Love for Love* (1695) represent more complex examples of this type. Maskwell achieves the "low" estimate of human nature on which his double dealing is based through Hobbesian introspection: "When each, who searches strictly his own mind/ May so much Fraud and Power of Baseness find" (II.i).[5] Scandal, an unprincipled libertine, is attempting to have a love affair with the astrologer's wife, Mrs. Foresight. His philosophy concerning mankind is clearly Hobbesian in origin: "I believe some Women are Vertuous too; but 'tis as I believe some Men are Valiant, thro' fear — For why shou'd a Man court Danger, or a Woman shun Pleasure?" (III. i). In such contexts as these, Hobbism became a rationalization for villainy. Indeed, much of the dramatic vigor and complexity of the libertines, rebels, and tyrants of the Restoration theater may derive from their Hobbist outlook.

Unquestionably, much of the anti-Hobbist animus observable among Hobbes's contemporaries can be ascribed to suspicions about the moral implications of this thought. A protest against the individualism attributed to Hobbes may be seen in the unpublished *Prose Characters* of Samuel Butler where the character of a "Modern Politician" is ironically portrayed in Hobbist terms. Butler's modern politician:

stedfastly believes, that all Men are born in the State of War, and that the civil Life is but a Cessation, and no Peace, nor Accommodation: And though all open Acts of Hostility are forborn by Consent, the Enmity continues and all Advantages by Treachery or Breach of Faith are very lawful — That there is no Difference between Virtue and Fraud among Friends, as well Enemies; nor any thing unjust, that a Man can do without Damage to his own Safety or Interest — That Oaths are but Springes to catch Woodcocks withal; and bind none but those, that are too weak and feeble to break them, when they become ever so small an Impediment to their Advantages.[6]

Butler's irony makes clear the extent to which "Hobbism" was perceived during the Restoration as a threat to the traditional values of interdependence. The modern politician who paid no heed to older patterns of family and community life would encourage the breaking up of these patterns in a society without beliefs, where pride and ambition reigned and corruption went unchecked.

This distrust of "Hobbism" is also central to Jonathan Swift's early satiric writings where he deals with "numerous and gross corruptions in Religion and Learning." In the opening paragraph of *The Battle of the Books,* for example, Swift directs his gift for parody against "modern writers on the politicks." Describing a "Republic of Dogs" in which "the Right of Possession" lies "in common," the first-person speaker of Swift's work reports that "Jealousies and Suspicions do so abound that the whole commonwealth of that street is reduced to a manifest *State of War*, of every *Citizen* against every *Citizen*, till some One of more Courage, Conduct or Fortune than the rest, seizes and enjoys the Prize; upon which naturally arises Plenty of Heartburning, and Envy, and Snarling against the *Happy Dog*."[7] Swift disliked philosophical systems generally, but it was his endeavor to redress the balance of mixed government which had been upset by the absolutism of modern philosophers that made him, like Butler, a severe critic of Hobbism. But Swift's ridicule of Hobbes is more comprehensive than Butler's, for, as Phillip Harth has shown, his satire on "the abuses of religion" in *A Tale of a Tub* makes use of many of the polemical themes of Hobbes's clerical opponents during the Restoration.[8] These divines were concerned less with Hobbes's political doctrines than with the allegedly atheistic implications of his materialism.[9] Their belief in Christianity depended heavily upon accepting innate ideas — especially the distinct idea of an immaterial God — as evidence, rather than resting simply upon faith, and they were firmly opposed to a thorough-going empiricism that made experience the sole source of human knowledge. Written between 1694 and 1696 when the fury of clerical opposition to Hobbes's empiricism had passed its peak, *A Tale of the Tub* is still the most devastating satire on the empiricist outlook. The famous section on the tailor-worshippers in section two, for example, uses religious imagery to suggest the kinship of empiricists with the fops of the "grande monde" — because they can find no place in their system for anything else but "the films and images that fly off upon their senses from the superfices of things." As a brilliant coda to Anglican polemics against Hobbism, *A Tale of a Tub* marks the end of a phase in which Hobbes's influence on English literature was mirrored primarily in opposition to his thought.

## II  *Influence on the Court Wits*

Hobbes's adversaries placed particular stress upon the impact of his ideas upon the traditional center of political authority in the kingdom — the court. Insisting upon seeing Hobbes as the source of the widespread skepticism and naturalistic temper of the age, they ascribed the indecent behavior of courtiers and wits to Hobbes's free-thinking opinions. According to Charles Wolseley, "Irreligion 'tis true in its practice hath been still the companion of every Age, but its open and publick defence seems the peculiar of this." And the same clergyman later adds that "most of the bad Principles of this Age are of no earlier date [then] one very ill Book, are indeed but the spawn of the Leviathan."[10]

From the available evidence, however, we might hazard the conclusion that members of Charles's entourage were licentious, not by intellectual conviction, but by inclination and opportunity.[11] Undoubtedly, the King's generous protection of his former tutor contributed to the relatively sympathetic reception which greeted Hobbes at court, but his ideas were never wholly accepted there. In any event, his political thought was adamantly opposed to egoism and license. Indeed, his own view of the scandalous activities of Charles's courtiers was clearly expressed in his objection to the works of some "comique" dramatists who "by conversation with Ill People have been able to present Vices upon the State more ridiculously and immodestly, by which they take their Rabble."[12]

The influence of Hobbes at court is best seen in the verse of the court wits, a circle of gifted if unstable poets and dramatists which included George Villiers, Duke of Buckingham, Charles Sackville, Earl of Dorset, Sir Charles Sedley, Sir George Etherege, William Wycherley, Sir George Savile, and Rochester. In the course of their development as poets, they assimilated Hobbes's empiricism to a libertine outlook in a way which he himself had clearly not envisaged. Hobbes's psychology taught that "sense ... properly so called must necessarily have in it a perpetual variety of phantasms, that they may be discerned one from another" (EW, I, 394). The effect of Hobbes's teaching upon the court wits, according to Wolseley, was to "secure" them "against their own guilt."[13] However, the more immediate reaction to the demand for variety in Hobbesian psychology was not so much security as uneasiness. Confronted by the necessity of renewing the sensations which give him the feeling of his own existence, the speaker of a song by Dorset discovers that the boredom of "many tedious Days" lies in wait for himself and his mistress if they do not "improve/A thousand diff'rent Ways./Those few short Moments snatch'd by Love."[14] The court wits probably owed to Hobbes this perception of time as a sequence of discontinuous moments, without continuity or change. The persistent application they made of this seemingly simple idea may help to explain their stress upon variety, unexpectedness, and inconstancy and also throw light upon their preference for slight and unpretentious verse forms: occasional poems, songs, epigrams, and lampoons.

How libertinism and Hobbesian psychology meshed to produce a disquieting effect can be seen most vividly in the poetry of Rochester. Although the extent to which Hobbes's thought actually influenced Rochester's poetry is a matter of dispute, there can be no doubt of its impact upon his greatest lyric, "Love and Life, A Song," which has a precise source in Hobbes's discussion of time in *Leviathan*. [15] In this poem Rochester pursues the implications of Hobbes's empiricism to their furthest extreme. Instead of simply endorsing the usual demand for sexual license, the poet sees inconstancy as an inevitable, even unfortunate, consequence of time and change. An awareness of the passing of time has taken on the force of inescapable necessity in his mind; it is the power that compels him to insist that man must seize "this livelong minute" because that is "all that heaven allows." Hobbes's influence on Rochester's Juvenalian "Satyr against Reason and Mankind" is less apparent, but the *persona's* distrust of purely speculative ideas, his conviction that fear is a mainspring of human action and, most importantly, his unsparing assault on human knavery and pettiness, may all derive something from different aspects of Hobbes's thought, especially his pessimistic view of human nature.[16] Of one thing we can be certain: the philosophical conclusions of a "Satyr against Reason and Mankind" are much too bleak to sustain any poet for long, and thus lend an air of plausibility to the apocryphal story, circulated by Bishop Gilbert Burnet, that during a dramatic death-bed conversion to Christianity Rochester should ascribe the errors of his life and writings to "that absurd and foolish Philosophy, which the world so much admired, propagated by the late Mr. Hobbs and others."[17]

If Hobbes's "low" view of human nature led to Rochester's misanthropic pessimism, it also may have influenced the lighter wit and gaiety as well as the irony and insight of such comedies as Etherege's *The Man of Mode* and Wycherley's *The Country Wife.* Like Rochester, these dramatists perceive life as pervaded by mistrust and suspicion. The true character of the relations between the sexes is portrayed as a struggle for domination by the stronger of the two. The clashes between Dorimant, Mrs. Loveit, and Harriet, between the Pinchwifes and the Fidgets, between Harcourt, Sparkish, and Alithea, as well as the indefatigable doings of Horner, all testify to the same truth. All regard life in society to be a form of covert warfare, in which the strong live by triumphing over the weak, if not for survival, then for pleasure, power, or just vanity. With certain qualifications, this image is common in early Restoration comedy. Lovers, friends, parents, and strangers — all may become each other's dupes. Hence wit serves as much for defense as offense: the principal characters of these comedies prefer politeness to disdain, similitude to direct statement, veiled expression to outright insult. By contrast, the character who confides, threatens or laughs outright is not to be trusted: he is a fool or person of unreliable character. Sparkish, Pinchwife, Fidget, Sir Fopling Flutter, or Mrs. Loveit are likely to disclose secrets or to display explosive violence or abject cowardice in dangerous situations. In their openness, the distance between one man and another, which creates a measure of mutual respect or security, has disappeared. Like the vainglorious in Hobbes's state of nature, they are at the mercy of others.

Etherege and Wycherley may have felt, like Rochester, that to live this way is to compound the human scandal of cowardice, irrationality, and hypocrisy. In their comedies, however, they are closer to the perspective of the detached spectator than to Rochester's intense moral indignation. Indeed, *The Man of Mode* and *The Country Wife* only confirm the inability of society to restrain the behavior of such offenders as are beyond the reach of laws and punishments. In these plays, vice and immorality are never entirely subdued, and natural warfare never really comes to an end. To a generation confident of its social institutions, Restoration comedy might suggest what Charles Lamb later described as a "Utopia of Gallantry" with "no reference whatever to the world that is"[18] — but the failure of the comic dramatists of the Restoration to present a convincing picture of how a world of seeming immorality is governed by a just social order may help to explain why contemporaries were ready to attribute the excesses of their plays to an imperfect understanding of Hobbes's ideas.


### III   *Hobbes and the New Economic Attitudes*

Not surprisingly, Hobbes made slower headway in the city than at court. His thought — which aroused violent opposition from Anglican clergymen — was not accepted by dissenters either. Recently, however, one critic has contended that there is a close correspondence between the Hobbesian state of nature and the competitive, market society of his age.[19] Significantly, Hobbes first gained sympathetic consideration in the city among the mercantile economists — William Petty, Josiah Child, and Charles Davenant.[20] Although there is little evidence of Hobbes's specific influence on these writers, they may have seen his notion of "natural" man motivated by rational self-interest rather than by morality or religion as a justification for their new economic attitudes. The clearest evidence of such a link appears in Bernard Mandeville's witty, iconoclastic poem *The Grumbling Hive, or Knaves turn'd Honest* (1705). In asserting that luxury and vice, though they might indeed be evil, are the source of man's prosperity, Mandeville clearly adopts a pessimistic view of human nature, not very different from Hobbes's. In "The Moral" to *The Grumbling Hive,* Mandeville stated as an axiom:

> T'enjoy the World's Conveniences,
> Be fam'd in War, yet live in Ease,
> Without great Vices, is a vain
> Eutopia seated in the Brain;

He adds for emphasis that "Fraud, Luxury and Pride must live,/ While we the Benefits receive."[21] Yet, it would be difficult to imagine a clearer example than these lines of the difference between Hobbes's ideas and those of his successors. Where Hobbes viewed man's unbridled egoism as a source of conflict that, if unchecked, could lead to anarchy, Mandeville maintained that not only self-interest but even private "vices" lead to public benefits.[22]

If Hobbes was not a prophet of economic individualism, did not his theory of man's natural state, at least provide a model for a competitive, market society? An answer to this question may be provided by Daniel Defoe who while deploring Hobbes's religious views proclaimed him "an exalted spirit in philosophy."[23] Defoe's indebtedness to Hobbes is best illustrated iń *Robinson Crusoe* which has been characterized as a paradigm of the solitary man dwelling in the state of nature. The island on which Crusoe is marooned — the sole survivor of a terrible shipwreck — is a setting outside history, far removed from the social and political institutions of man. Here Defoe acknowledges the vulnerability of civilized man "reduced to a mere state of nature." As the novel quickly enough makes us aware, Crusoe's mind is dominated by the fear of sudden destruction. On the other hand, the novel also suggests that the fear he describes is largely imaginary: after an initial period of panic, he settles down to constructive, peaceful tasks: tilling, manufacturing, building, and tending his goats. But as soon as he discovers the footprint in the sand, he reverts to a condition of "brutal solitude" in which he dwells "in the constant Snare of the Fear of Man," abandoning his projects and devoting his energies instead to self-defense.[24]

Crusoe's career raises the question of whether the novel evidences Hobbes's influence in shaping Defoe's economic attitudes. Some support for this view might be drawn from the example of Crusoe's servant Friday and the sailors whose subjection by covenant and written contract enables Crusoe to undertake some of his most ambitious projects. On the other hand, Crusoe's notion of an "idyll of individual enterprise" free of competitors[25] is only a dream. Lacking the aid of his fellow men and the security of covenants and laws, he lives in a state of perpetual uncertainty; he embodies the novelist's warning of the terrors that await men in the state of nature. The influence of Hobbes thus appears to place *Robinson Crusoe* largely within a political rather than an economic tradition.

## IV    *Hobbes's Later Influence*

Hobbes's subsequent reputation and influence can be viewed as inversely proportional to the resistance engendered by his ideas. Hobbes's contemporary critics, as we have seen, were not exactly noted for their sense of proportion, restraint, or critical exactitude. On the contrary, they succeeded in conferring on almost every aspect of his thought a mythology equal to the threat it posed to society. As a result, *Leviathan* soon became for many Englishmen a creature of imagination rather than an actual book. The evidence of its decline in popularity can be seen in the fact that, while it went through several editions in his own lifetime, it was published only once during the eighteenth century.[26] In spite of this decline, however, some of Hobbes's ideas continued to exert an influence even if only indirectly. In general, Hobbes's doctrine of corporeal body, his speculations on space and time, and his metaphysics of motion failed to obtain acceptance by Englishmen during the eighteenth century; even before the advent of Newton, Hobbes's attempts at geometry and physics carried little conviction. Dryden's jibe that Hobbes began studying mathematics "when it was too late" shows the depths to which Hobbes's reputation had fallen as a result of his controversies with John Wallis, Seth Ward, and others.[27] A similar fate befell Hobbes's pronouncements on scientific method. Many writers shared his distrust of existing learning and his belief in the importance of mathematics as a model of rational thought. But his preference for framing wide and far-reaching hypotheses about nature-in-general rather than gathering empirical data for particular experiments had little impact upon eighteenth-century poets, virtuosi, and researchers to whom the founding of the Royal Society in 1662 had come as a golden opportunity.

Many Englishmen who could not accept his metaphysics or methodology did, however, agree with his assumption that sovereignty is unitary and absolute. But even this doctrine ceased to hold the interest of serious thinkers after the Glorious Revolution. The political views of Sir William Temple, Henry St. John, Viscount Bolingbroke, Swift, and others can be seen as modern versions of the classical theory of mixed sovereignty against which Hobbes had waged unceasing warfare.[28] During the eighteenth century, Hobbes's political heritage came increasingly to consist largely of the maxim that without a common power to overawe us all ''Government it self at length must fall/To Nature's state; where all have Right to all.''[29]

On the other hand, Hobbes's account of the poetic process, with its special stress on the natural workings of the human mind, had a lasting influence as a positive doctrine. Hence, even though Hobbes's metaphysical beliefs were violently attacked by many of his contemporaries, his critical vocabulary and psychology became, in the words of J. E. Spingarn, ''the groundwork of Restoration criticism.''[30] It is true that none of the major critics of the late seventeenth and eighteenth centuries adopted views identical with Hobbes's. But the theories of Charleton, Dryden, Locke, Temple, Addison, and others can be seen as the elaboration of Hobbes's distinctions between fancy and judgment. Even as late as the end of the eighteenth century, Hobbes's conception of the fancy continued to hold the attention of such critics as Samuel Taylor Coleridge — if chiefly as a worthy antagonist against which the romantic theory of imagination should be measured.

Hobbes was not only remembered as a defender of absolutism or as the founder of a psychological school of criticism. Later philosophers remembered him for the questions he raised concerning the mind's operations. These thinkers (including Locke, George Berkeley, and David Hume) dissociated themselves from Hobbes's assumption that philosophy should be concerned with causal explanation rather than exact description. But the impetus given by Hobbes to the development of a theory of knowledge was, indeed, one of the principle ways in which he exercised a powerful, if oblique, influence on later philosophers. Hobbes's empiricism, nominalism, and skepticism became a major focus of attention in the eighteenth century, even if his legacy consisted largely of the formulation of fundamental questions to which his metaphysics provided no plausible answers.

In the nineteenth century, Hobbes received attention chiefly from the utilitarians, not only for the intrinsic merit of his thought, but, perhaps more importantly, because Hobbes was viewed as an early exponent of a secular and naturalistic doctrine similar to their own. It is not surprising, therefore, that the one major edition of his works during the nineteenth century was planned and completed by two members of the school, George Grote and Sir William Molesworth. Hobbes himself was not a utilitarian; nor did he believe that moral values should be assessed in terms of their contribution to general happiness. But it should be added that the psychological hedonism and ethical calculus of such writers as Jeremy Bentham and James Mill has at least an indirect connection with Hobbes's ethical and political thought through its link with critics of Hobbes who, in opposing his ideas, adopted some of his assumptions.

By contrast with the limited appeal of Hobbes's writings in the nineteenth century, his ideas have stimulated a wide range of interest among students of philosophy and literature during the twentieth century, from both a historical and an ahistorical perspective. Historically, Hobbes has been recognized by modern commentators as one of the initiators of the dramatic revision in philosophy that accompanied the attempt to bring specifically human concerns into harmony with the materialistic, mechanistic and deterministic outlook of modern science. In this context, however, the modern appeal of Hobbes's thought is not that it presented a scientific antithesis to an older and increasingly outmoded humanism. Such a dichotomy actually obscures more than it reveals about Hobbes's historical significance. Rather, in an age in which humanism was coming to be perceived as irrelevant to man's concerns, Hobbes's thought attempted an original synthesis of rational analysis with a humanistic program for the renewal of the body politic.

On the other hand, Hobbes's theories of moral and political obligation still invite prolific ahistorical discussion. Hobbes was an empiricist who tested all norms by their relevance to experience; he was a rationalist with an almost Euclidean vision of the internal self-sufficiency of any truly rigorous logical argument; and he was a skeptic who doubted the capacity of any man to possess the truth with certainty. Hobbes's theory of rights and obligations encompasses these diverse elements; hence it is a weaving together, with marvellous subtlety, of strains which in other philosophers might appear as logically independent. Making it possible for modern commentators to emphasize divergent, even conflicting, aspects of

Hobbes's political theory, this subtlety is unmistakable evidence of his philosophical acumen. It is also the source of the recurrent and permanent appeal of his thought.

# Notes and References

## Chapter One

1. *Thomae Hobbes Malmesburiensis, Vita carmina expressa,* trans. Benjamin Farrington, *Rationalist Annual,* 1958, pp. 22–31. References to this translation in my text are to line number. There are two other original accounts of Hobbes's life: *Thomae Hobbae Malmesburiensis, Vita,* composed in Latin prose by Hobbes himself and *Vitae Hobbianae Auctarium,* written in Latin by Hobbes's admirer, Richard Blackbourne, M.D. All three Latin accounts are published in *Thomae Hobbes Malmesburiensis — Opera Philosophica Quae Latini Scripsit,* ed. Sir William Molesworth (London, 1845), I, ix–xcix. Subsequent references to this edition in my text are to the abbreviation *L W,* volume and page number.

2. *Aubrey's Brief Lives,* ed. by Oliver Lawson Dick (Ann Arbor, Michigan, 1962), p. 147. Subsequent references in my text are to page number. Dick's edition was first published in 1949. Aubrey's life of Hobbes is the longest and most carefully researched of the *Brief Lives.* In addition there are numerous references to Hobbes in the other lives.

3. Thomas F. Fuller, *The History of the Worthies of England* (London, 1840), III, 287.

4. George Croom Robertson, *Hobbes* (London, 1886), p. 21.

5. *A Short Tract on First Principles* was published as an appendix to *The Elements of Law,* ed. Ferdinand Tönnies (London, 1889).

6. *The English Works of Thomas Hobbes,* ed. Sir William Molesworth (London, 1839–1845), IV, 414. Subsequent references in my text are to the abbreviation EW, volume and page number.

7. John Wallis in EW, IV, 413; and Clarendon, *A Brief View and Survey of Hobbes's Errors* (Oxford, 1676), p. 317; both cited by John Laird, *Hobbes* (London, 1934), p. 15.

8. Cited by Laird, p. 17.

9. For a discussion of Hobbes's influence on the English de facto theorists, see Quentin Skinner, "Conquest and Consent: Thomas Hobbes and the Engagement Controversy," in *The Interregnum: the Quest for Settlement, 1646–1660,* ed. G. E. Aylmer (Hamden, Conn., 1972), 79–98.

10. "Six Lessons to the Savilian Professor of Mathematics" (EW, VII, 181–356).

11. See the mention of arrears in payment in Hobbes's undated petition to the King, EW, VII, 471–472.

12. Thomas White was a Catholic priest who was persecuted in England for the opinions he published in several controversial tracts.

13. Quoted by Robertson, pp. 193–194.

14. *Historiae et Antiquitatis Universitatis Oxoniensis* (Oxford, 1674), II, 449.

15. Ormonde Papers, H.M.C. N.S. IV., 13th December, 1679, cited by Laird, p. 31.

## Chapter Two

1. See J. H. Hexter, "The Education of the Aristocracy in the Renaissance," in *Reappraisals in History* (London, 1961), 45–70.

2. On the conventions of humanist history during the Renaissance, see Felix Gilbert, *Machiavelli and Guicciardini, Politics and History in Sixteenth-Century Florence* (Princeton, N.J., 1965), pp. 203–235. The fullest discussion of Hobbes's humanist conception of history is by Leo Strauss, *The Political Philosophy of Thomas Hobbes* (Oxford, 1936), pp. 79–107.

3. For a discussion of the thesis that Hobbes's political thought is independent of his philosophical premises, see Robertson, p. 57; and Strauss. The position taken here is not that the "essential content" of Hobbes's political theory was already embodied in his translation of Thucydides' *History* (Strauss, p. 112). Rather it is that the special prudential ethical form which his conceptions took was shaped by his awareness of what he took to be the relevance of his theory for the conduct of politics. This philosopher and scientist was first of all a dedicated humanist. His impulse was always to employ logical arguments as evidence of the need for peace.

4. References to *The Elements of Law* in my text are to part, chapter, and section.

5. EW, VII, p. 468. References to *A Short Tract* in my text are to section and principle or conclusion. Watkins discusses *A Short Tract* within the context of the mechanical tradition. In my view the parallels between Hobbes's scientific theories in *A Short Tract* and Renaissance thought are more fundamental and revealing. See Watkins, pp. 22–27.

6. Hobbes defines what he calls "Conveniency, or Disconveniency and the Greekes, Sympathy and Antipathy," to be the "worke" of agents and patients "proper to their Species," which Hobbes again explains by the example of the lodestone (II, Conc. 9).

7. Watkins, p. 26.

## Chapter Three

1. James Harrington, *Prerogative of Popular Government,* I, 8; Joseph Addison, *Spectator,* No. 47, April 24, 1711; Denis Diderot, *Oeuvres completes,* ed. Jules Assézat and Maurice Tourneaux (Paris, 1875–1879), III, 466.
2. René Descartes, *Meditations on First Philosophy,* Meditation I.
3. On the difference between Hobbes's ethics and Aristotle's, see Thomas A. Spragens, Jr., *The Politics of Motion, The World of Thomas Hobbes* (Lexington, Kentucky, 1973), pp. 53–72.
4. For an interesting analysis of Hobbes's conception of power, see S. I. Benn, "Hobbes on Power," in *Hobbes and Rousseau, A Collection of Critical Essays,* ed. Maurice Cranston and Richard S. Peters (Garden City, New York, 1972), pp. 184–212.
5. Strauss, pp. 35–43.
6. For extensive discussion of the nature and history of treatises on the passions, see Anthony Levi, S. J., *French Moralists The Theory of the Passions, 1585–1649* (Oxford, 1964).
7. See the usage in I, 17, 14 and I, 18, 11.
8. A. E. Taylor, "The Ethical Doctrine of Hobbes," repr. in *Hobbes's Leviathan: Interpretation and Criticism,* ed. Bernard H. Baumrin (Belmont, California, 1969), pp. 36–37.
9. Howard Warrender, *The Political Philosophy of Thomas Hobbes* (Oxford, 1957), p. 93.
10. Sir Leslie Stephen, *Hobbes* (London, 1904), p. 192.
11. Hobbes's political theory has been examined by many scholars. Besides the works of Strauss, Warrender, and Watkins, already cited, see the important discussions in M. M. Goldsmith, *Hobbes's Science of Politics* (New York, 1966); F. C. Hood, *The Divine Politics of Thomas Hobbes* (London, 1964); M. Oakeshott, *Rationalism in Politics and Other Essays* (New York, 1962).
12. Howard Warrender, "Hobbes's Conception of Morality," repr. in Baumrin, p. 67.
13. Warrender, p. 318.

## Chapter Four

1. Jean Jacques Rousseau, *A Discourse on the Origin of Inequality,* trans. G. D. H. Cole (London, Toronto, and New York, 1913), p. 175.
2. For a sophisticated variation of this argument from a Marxist perspective, see C. B. Macpherson, *The Political Theory of Possessive Individualism* (Oxford, 1962), pp. 9–106.
3. Watkins has presented perhaps the most persuasive argument for viewing Hobbes's laws of nature as prudential rather than moral by noting

that they conform to what Kant called assertoric hypothetical imperatives, that is commands akin to doctor's orders. See Watkins, pp. 55–57.

4. For accounts which emphasize the importance of moral obligation in Hobbes's account of the laws of nature, see A. E. Taylor, "The Ethical Doctrine of Thomas Hobbes," ed. cit., pp. 35–48. The Taylor thesis was greatly developed, with some modifications, by Howard Warrender, *The Political Philosophy of Hobbes* (ed. cit.), and by F. C. Hood, *The Divine Politics of Thomas Hobbes, An Interpretation of Leviathan* (Oxford, 1964). For a valuable survey of the many complexities of this problem, see W. H. Greenleaf, "Hobbes: The Problem of Interpretation," in *Hobbes and Rousseau,* ed. cit., pp. 8–17.

5. A striking feature of Hobbes's account is that the natural right of self-preservation always refers to the individual, while the laws of nature are rules for the preservation of men in general. This distinction led Howard Warrender to suggest that for Hobbes a law of nature does not mean "preserve yourself" but rather "act so that all men can be preserved, except where this is inconsistent." "Hobbes's Conception of Morality," in Baumrin, p. 78.

6. The passage is cited by A. E. Taylor, "The Ethical Doctrine of Hobbes," in Baumrin, p. 37.

7. The distinction between the desire for immediate benefits and the desire for self-preservation appears to be of Stoic origin. See Diogenes Laertius' "Life of Zeno," *The Essential Works of Stoicism,* ed. Moses Hadas (New York, 1961), p. 25.

8. In a footnote to *De Cive,* II, i, Hobbes makes it clear that, while he does not regard reason as "an infallible faculty," he does not believe that reason serves to justify the passions. Right reason, for Hobbes, is not divine "ratio" or divine law, but the reasoning of every individual human being "concerning those actions of his which may either redound to the damage or benefit of his neighbors" (EW, II, 16). It is clear that although reason retains its normative character in opposing the passions, it is not infallible being always subject to the sway of passion. Indeed it might be possible for a person acting from "true principles" to reason falsely, for Hobbes later insists that "no man but may be deceived in reasoning" (EW, II, 220). Hobbes's entire discussion, however, seems calculated to avoid giving this impression.

9. Hobbes argues that the ten commandments command "implicitly" as laws of nature, but how "implicit" commands differ from "explicit" commands is not made clear.

## Chapter Five

1. F. C. Hood; F. S. McNeilly, *The Anatomy of Leviathan* (New

York, 1968); David P. Gauthier, *The Logic of Leviathan: The Moral and Political Theory* (Oxford, Clarendon Press, 1969).

2. See Laird, p. 16.

3. Macpherson, pp. 9-107.

4. Hood, *passim.*

5. Watkins, p. 140. Hobbes's statement that one universal name is imposed on many things "for their similitude in some quality, or other accident" (EW, III, 21) is seen by Watkins as a retreat from extreme nominalism to a version of Aristotle's theory of universals, pp. 147, 148. For a useful general introduction to the entire subject, see Hilary Staniland, *Universals* (Garden City, New York, 1972).

6. Dorothy Van Ghent, *The English Novel: Form and Function* (New York, Harper Torchbook, 1961), p. 39.

7. See Levi, pp. 19-20, for a discussion of this distinction.

8. In *A Short Tract* (Sect. 3., Conc., 3-7), Hobbes establishes an implicit parallel between moral values and sense data, both of which are thought to inhere in the mind rather than in objects.

9. Bernard Gert, "Hobbes and Psychological Egoism," *JHI,* XXVIII (1967), pp. 503-520; see also McNeilly, pp. 96-110, for a similar conclusion.

10. Macpherson, pp. 46-70.

11. See Jean G. Peristiany, *Honor and Shame: the Values of Mediterranean Societies,* (Chicago, 1965), for convincing analyses of how honor can proximate competitive display in societies whose values are clearly precapitalist. The most detailed critique of the Macpherson thesis is William Letwin's "The Economic Foundation of Hobbes's Politics," in *Hobbes and Rousseau,* pp. 143-164. For a comprehensive survey of all of Hobbes's comments on society, see Keith Thomas, "The Social Origins of Hobbes's Political Thought," in *Hobbes Studies,* 185-236.

12. See Hood, p. 48.

13. On the importance of this distinction, see Bernard Gert, *Man and Citizen* (Garden City, New York, Anchor paperback, 1972), p. 18.

14. See the pertinent comment of Stewart Hampshire on John Rawls's *A Theory of Justice* (Cambridge, Mass., 1972), "The objection can be made ... that a blind chooser might, not irrationally, just choose to gamble, and prefer a society where the winner takes all, or virtually all; he may prefer to take the risk of being a slave if he has a chance of being a master." (*New York Review of Books,* Feb. 24, 1972), p. 37.

15. For the suggestion that the state of nature was never the condition of an entire species for Hobbes, but rather the moment when a previously existing political society is on the verge of dissolution into civil war, see Sheldon Wolin, *Politics and Vision* (Boston, 1960), pp. 262-265.

16. According to John M. Steadman, in "Leviathan and Renaissance Etymology," *JHI,* 28 (1967), pp. 575-576, Hobbes, in applying leviathan

to the state and its head, was following a minor exegetical tradition in the scriptural criticism of the seventeenth century. Most commentators, however, glossed leviathan as a symbol of the devil, a point which Hobbes's opponents did not fail to exploit.

17. Quoted by Mintz, p. 56.

18. Mintz, p. 12.

19. On this point, see Ronald Hepburn, "Hobbes on the Knowledge of God," in *Hobbes and Rousseau,* pp. 99–100.

20. *Ibid.,* p. 105.

21. Strauss, p. 199. For the most thorough defense of Hobbes's sincerity in religious matters, see William B. Glover, "God and Thomas Hobbes," in *Hobbes Studies,* pp. 141–149.

## Chapter Six

1. For examples of the attitude that Hobbes's thinking about the poetic process was motivated by a distrust of the imagination, see Paul Spencer Wood, "The Opposition to Neo-Classicism in England between 1660 and 1700," *PMLA,* 43 (1928), 182–197; George Williamson, "The Restoration Revolt Against Enthusiasm," *SP,* 30 (1930), 571–603; and Donald F. Bond, "Distrust of Imagination in English Neo-Classicism," *PQ,* 14 (1935), 54–69.

2. *The Poetics,* trans. Leon Golden (Englewood Cliffs, N.J., 1968), p. 41.

3. Josephine Miles, "Toward a Theory of Style and Change," *JAAC,* 22 (1963), p. 64.

## Chapter Seven

1. *Hobbes and His Critics* (London, 1951).

2. *The Hunting of Leviathan* (Cambridge, Mass., 1962).

3. "The Ideological Context of Hobbes's Political Thought," *The Historical Journal,* IX (1966), 286–317; "Thomas Hobbes and His Disciples in France and England," *Comparative Studies in Society and History,* VIII (1966), pp. 153–167.

4. *The Works of John Tillotson,* ed. Thomas Burch (London, 1820), I, 418.

5. Citations of Congreve's comedies enclosed within parentheses in my text are to *The Complete Plays of William Congreve,* ed. Herbert Davis (Chicago, 1967).

6. *The Genuine Remains in Verse & Prose,* ed. R. Thyer (London, 1759), II, p. 6.

7. *A Tale of a Tub, To which is Added The Battle of the Books and*

*The Mechanical Operation of the Spirit*, ed. A. C. Guthkelch and D. Nichol Smith (Oxford, 1958), p. 219. The source of Swift's parody of Hobbes in these passages may be Eachard's travesty of Hobbes's famous comparison of human societies with the societies of ants and bees, *Some Opinions of Mr. Hobbes Considered in a Second Dialogue between Philautus and Timothy* (London, 1673), L3–L5. For evidence of Swift's acquaintance with Eachard's writings, see R. C. Elliott, "Swift and Dr. Eachard," *PMLA,* LXIX (1954), 1250–1257.

8. *Swift and Anglican Rationalism* (Chicago, 1961), pp. 83–85; 145–148; 151–153.

9. See Mintz, p. vii. An excellent recent discussion of Hobbes's influence on Swift is Alan S. Fisher's "An End to the Renaissance: Erasmus, Hobbes and *The Tale of a Tub*," *HLQ,* XXXVIII (1974), 1–20.

10. Charles Wolseley, *The Reasonableness of Scripture-Belief* (London, 1672; facs. reprod., New York, 1973), sq. A–4.

11. A point excellently made by Mintz, pp. 138–142.

12. A letter to the Duchess of Newcastle, 9 February 1661, in Margaret Cavendish, *A Collection of Letters and Poems* (London, 1678), p. 67.

13. Wolseley, sq. A–4.

14. *The Works of Celebrated Authors, Of Whose Writings there are but small Remains* (London, 1750), I, 207.

15. Jeremy Treglown, "The Satiric Inversion of Some English Sources in Rochester's Poetry," *RES,* New Ser. XXIV (1973), p. 44.

16. See especially Thomas H. Fujimura, "Rochester's 'Satyr against Mankind," An Analysis," *SP,* 55 (1958), 576–590.

17. Robert Parsons, *A Sermon Preached at the Funeral of the Rt Honorable John Earl of Rochester* (Oxford, 1680), p. 26.

18. "On the Artificial Comedy of the Last Age," in *The Idea of Comedy,* ed. W. K. Wimsatt (Englewood Cliffs, New Jersey, 1969), p. 217.

19. Macpherson, pp. 42–69.

20. For evidence of Hobbes's impact on these writers, see Maximillian E. Novak, *Economics and the Fiction of Daniel Defoe* (Berkeley and Los Angeles, 1962), p. 162.

21. *The Fable of the Bees,* ed. F. B. Kaye (Oxford, 1925), I, 36.

22. On this point, see Frederick Copleston, S. J., *A History of Philosophy* (Garden City, New York, 1964), V, I, pp. 189, 210. Hobbes's opposition to the doctrine of the natural harmony of interests, which is central to the ideology of economic individualism, is bluntly put in his comparison of human societies with the societies of bees and ants. In the latter, "the common good differeth not from the private." On the other hand, man "can relish nothing but what is eminent" (EW, III, 156).

23. *The Storm* (London, 1704), p. 4; cited in Novak, p. 34.

24. Hobbes's influence on *Robinson Crusoe* is discussed in Maximillian

E. Novak's excellent study *Defoe and the Nature of Man* (Oxford, 1963), pp. 33-35.

25. Ian Watt, "*Robinson Crusoe* as a Myth," *Essays in Criticism*, I (1951), p. 108.

26. On the publishing history of *Leviathan,* see Hugh MacDonald and Mary Hargreaves, *Thomas Hobbes, A Bibliography (London, 1952), pp. 27-36.*

27. *"Preface to 'Fables Ancient & Modern'*," in *The Poems of John Dryden,* ed. James Kinsley (Oxford, 1958), IV, 1448.

28. See Isaac Kramnick, *Bolingbroke and His Circle* (Cambridge, Mass., 1968), pp. 72-77; 137-152; 207-208.

29. Skinner, "The Ideological Context of Hobbes's Political Thought," pp. 298-299.

30. J. E. Spingarn, *Critical Essays of the Seventeenth Century* (Oxford, 1908-1909), I, xxvii-xxviii.

# Selected Bibliography

## PRIMARY SOURCES

The only major editions of Hobbes's works are *The English Works of Thomas Hobbes,* edited by Sir William Molesworth (11 vols., London, John Bohn, 1839–1845), and *Thomae Hobbes Malmesburiensis — Opera Philosophica quae Latine scripsit Omnia,* edited by Sir William Molesworth (5 vols., London, John Bohn, 1839–1845). These contain all the published writings and are referred to throughout this volume. Also consulted for quotations in my text is *The Elements of Law, Natural and Politic,* edited by Ferdinand Tönnies (Cambridge, Eng. Cambridge University Press, 1928; reprint New York, Barnes & Noble, 1969). Appendix I consists of a previously unpublished "Short Tract on First Principles."

These editions may be supplemented by the following works:

*Behemoth: or The Long Parliament,* edited for the first time from the original manuscript by Ferdinand Tönnies (Cambridge, Cambridge University Press, 1928).

*De Cive or the Citizen,* edited by S. P. Lamprecht (New York, Appleton, Century Crofts, Inc., 1949).

*Leviathan,* edited with an introduction by Michael Oakeshott (Oxford, Basil Blackwell, 1955).

*Man and Citizen,* edited with an introduction by Bernard Gert (New York, Doubleday & Co., 1972). This text includes the only English translation of *De Homine* (Chapters 10–15).

## SECONDARY SOURCES

BAUMRIN, BERNARD. *Hobbes's LEVIATHAN: Interpretation and Criticism.* Belmont, California: Wadsworth Publishing Company, 1969. Useful reprint of articles and extracts related to Hobbes's major work.

BRANDT, FRITHIOF. *Thomas Hobbes's Mechanical Conception of Nature.* Copenhagen: Levin & Munksgaard, 1928. The only full length study in English of Hobbes's ideas on science.

BROWN, KEITH. *Hobbes Studies.* Cambridge Massachusetts: Harvard University Press, 1965. Important collection of articles; especially valuable for its essays on Hobbes's political, social and religious thought.

167

BOWLE, JOHN. *Hobbes and His Critics: A Study in Seventeenth Century Constitutionalism.* London: Jonathan Cape, 1951. A survey of the contemporary reaction to Hobbes's political thought which sides with Hobbes's critics.

CRANSTON, MAURICE and PETERS, RICHARD. *Hobbes and Rousseau: A Collection of Critical Essays.* Garden City: Doubleday & Co., 1972. Stimulating collection of essays written especially for this volume.

FISHER, ALAN S. "An End to the Renaissance: Erasmus, Hobbes and *A Tale of a Tub*," *HLQ*, XXXVIII (1974), 1-20. Examines Hobbes's influence on Swift.

GAUTHIER, DAVID P. *The Logic of LEVIATHAN: The Moral and Political Theory of Thomas Hobbes,* Oxford, Clarendon Press, 1969. Argues that Hobbes's attempt to base a political theory of unlimited political authority upon unlimited individualism is a failure.

GERT, BERNARD. "Hobbes and Psychological Egoism," *JHI*, XXVIII (1967), 503-520. Challenges the traditional picture of Hobbes as a psychological egoist.

GOLDSMITH, M. M. *Hobbes's Science of Politics.* New York and London: Columbia University Press, 1966. Comprehensive, invaluable study of Hobbes's political thought in relation to his general philosophical system.

HILL, CHRISTOPHER. *Puritanism and Revolution: Studies in Interpretation of the English Revolution of the 17th Century.* London: Secker & Warburg, 1958. Includes a stimulating essay examining Hobbes's historical significance from a Marxist viewpoint.

HOOD, F. C. *The Divine Politics of Thomas Hobbes: An Interpretation of Leviathan.* Oxford: Clarendon Press, 1964. The most extreme statement of the view that Hobbes is basically a Christian moralist.

KING, PRESTON. *The Ideology of Order: A Comparative Analysis of Jean Bodin and Thomas Hobbes.* London: Allen & Unwin, 1974. Fullest discussion of the view that the norms upon which Hobbes's account of political authority is based are derived from facts, not values.

LAIRD, JOHN. *Hobbes.* London: Ernest Benn, 1934. Valuable introduction; contains some interesting parallels between Hobbes and medieval political thinkers.

MACDONALD, HUGH and HARGREAVES. *Thomas Hobbes, A Bibliography.* London: The Bibliographical Society, 1952. Standard bibliography of Hobbes's writings.

MCNEILLY, F. S. *The Anatomy of LEVIATHAN.* New York: St. Martin's Press, 1968. Valuable insights on the development of Hobbes's political thought from his early writings to *Leviathan.*

MACPHERSON, C. B. *The Political Theory of Possessive Individualism, Hobbes to Locke.* Oxford: Oxford University Press, 1962. Provoca-

tive, if controversial, approach to Hobbes from a Marxist
perspective.

MINTZ, SAMUEL I. *The Hunting of Leviathan: Seventeenth-Century Reactions to the Materialism and Moral Philosophy of Thomas Hobbes.*
Cambridge, England: Cambridge University Press, 1962. An indispensable introduction to the contemporary response to Hobbes's
thought.

OAKESHOTT, MICHAEL. *Hobbes on Civil Association.* Berkeley & Los
Angeles: The University of California Press, 1975. Incorporates into
one volume all of the author's writings on Hobbes including his seminal analyses of Hobbes's theory of obligation.

PETERS, RICHARD. *Hobbes.* Middlesex, England: Penguin Books, 1956.
Useful introduction; particularly valuable for its analysis of Hobbes's
psychology.

ROBERTSON, GEORGE CROOM. *Hobbes.* Edinburgh and London: William
Blackwood and Sons, 1890. Pioneering study of Hobbes's thought;
the first critic to argue that Hobbes worked out his political ideas
before he became a philosopher.

SCHOCHET, GORDON J. *Patriarchalism in Political Thought, The Authoritarian Family and Political Attitudes Especially in Seventeenth-Century England.* New York: Basic Books, 1975. Includes an excellent chapter on Hobbes's relation to the patriarchalist tradition.

SKINNER, QUENTIN. "Conquest and Consent: Thomas Hobbes and the
Engagement Controversy" in *The Interregnum: the Quest for Settlement, 1646–1660.* Ed. G. E. Aylmer (Hamden, Conn.: Archon
Books, 1972), 79–98. Important attempt to locate Hobbes's political
thought in a contemporary historical context.

_____. "Thomas Hobbes and his Disciples in France and England,"
*Comparative Studies in Society and History,* VIII (1966), 153–167.
Argues that Hobbes's contemporary reputation was more favorable
than has been generally supposed.

_____. "The Ideological Context of Hobbes's Political Thought,"
*The Historical Journal,* IX (1966), 286–317. Relates Hobbes's political writings to a specific tradition of seventeenth-century political
thought.

SRAGENS, THOMAS A., JR. *The Politics of Motion: The World of Thomas
Hobbes.* Lexington, Kentucky: The University Press of Kentucky,
1973. Tries to show that in spite of Hobbes's rejection of Aristotelian
orthodoxy, his general framework remained Aristotelian.

STEADMAN, JOHN M. "Leviathan and Renaissance Etymology," *JHI,* 28
(1967), 575–576. Traces the history of the term Leviathan in Renaissance Biblical exegesis.

STEPHEN, SIR LESLIE. *Hobbes.* London: Macmillan, 1904. General introduction by an early intellectual historian.

STRAUSS, LEO. *The Political Philosophy of Thomas Hobbes: Its Basis and Genesis.* Oxford: Clarendon Press, 1936. Complex, brilliant study of Hobbes's political thought; expands Robertson's thesis that Hobbes's political ideas were formed before his conversion to science and philosophy.

TAYLOR, A. E. "The Ethical Doctrine of Hobbes," *Philosophy,* xiii (1938), 406–424. Vastly influential article; asserted the thesis that Hobbes's ethical theory is logically independent of his psychology and is a strict moral theory which is not based upon prudence and self-interest.

_____, *Thomas Hobbes.* London: Archibald Constable, 1908. Brief but still valuable exposition of Hobbes's ideas.

THORPE, CLARENCE D. *The Aesthetic Theory of Thomas Hobbes.* Ann Arbor: University of Michigan Press, 1940. Important, lengthy study of Hobbes's critical thought; argues that Hobbes was the founder of a "psychological school of criticism" that culminated in Coleridge's theory of the imagination.

WARRENDER, HOWARD. *The Political Philosophy of Hobbes: His Theory of Obligation.* Oxford: Clarendon Press, 1957. Major study of Hobbes's theory of political obligation; expands the "Taylor thesis" that Hobbes's ethical doctrine has no necessary connection to his psychology.

WATKINS, J. W. N. *Hobbes's System of Ideas.* London: Hutchinson University Library, 1965; 2nd ed., 1973. The liveliest and most readable recent study of Hobbes's thought; views Hobbes's political theory as part of a unified system of ideas.

WOLIN, SHELDON. *Politics and Vision: continuity and innovation in Western political thought.* Boston: Little Brown, 1960. Contains an important chapter on Hobbes.

_____. *Hobbes and the Epic Tradition of Political Theory.* Los Angeles: The Clark Library, 1970. Imaginative discussion of the heroic elements in Hobbes's political writings, particularly *Leviathan*.

# Index

(The works of Hobbes are listed under his name)

*Absalom and Achitophel* (Dryden), 155
Addison, Joseph, 46, 155
Adhelm, 14
Ammianus Marcellinus, 17
Aristotle, 34
association of ideas, 49, 102-103
Athelstane, 14
Aubrey, John, 14, 29-30
Aytoun, Sir Robert, 18

Bacon, Francis, 17-18
Baillie, Robert, 124
*Ballistica* (Mersenne), 22
battle of Worcester, 23, 97
*Battle of the Books, The* (Swift), 148
Bentham, Jeremy, 156
Berigardus, Claudius, 20
Berkeley, George, 155
Borelli, Giovanni Alfonso, 129
Bowle, John, 146
Boyle, Robert, 30
Bramhall, John, Bishop of Derry, 23, 26-27
*Brief Lives* (Aubrey), 14-16, 18, 21, 27-28, 30-31
Bunyan, John, 80
Burnet, Gilbert, Bishop of Salisbury, 151
Butler, Joseph, Bishop of Bristol, 109

Camden, William, 17
Carey, Lucius, Lord Falkland, 21, 23
"Castigations of Hobbes's Animadversions" (Bramhall), 27
"Catching of Leviathan the Great Whale, The" (Bramhall), 27
Cavendish, William, Duke of Newcastle, 44

Cavendish, William, first Earl of Devonshire, 16, 18, 32-34, 54
Cavendish, William, second Earl of Devonshire, 16, 18, 32-34
Cavendish, William, third Earl of Devonshire, 18, 25, 30-31
Chapman, George, 17
Charles II, 23, 27-29, 96-97, 125
Charleton, Dr. Walter Charleton, 30, 155
Charlton, 14
Child, Josiah, 152
Chillingworth, William, 21
church and state, 71, 91-95, 125-26
Clinton, Sir Gervase, 18
*Cogitata Physico-Mathematica* (Mersenne), 22
Coleridge, Samuel Taylor, 155
*Constant Couple, The* (Farquhar), 147
Council of State, the, 23
*Country Wife, The* (Wycherley), 151-52
Cowley, Abraham, 133, 146
Crabbe, George, 135
Cromwell, Oliver, 24, 27, 96
Cromwell, Richard, 27

Davenant, Charles, 152
Davenant, Sir William, 133, 146
Davys, John, of Kidwelly, 26
Demosthenes, 34
*de facto* theorists, 24, 146, 159n9
"Defence of the True Liberty of Human Actions from Antecedent or Extrinsic Necessity" (Bramhall), 26
Defoe, Daniel, 106, 146, 153
*De Motu* (Galileo), 74
*De Motus Cordis* (Harvey), 74
Derbyshire, 25

Descartes, René, 18-20, 39, 46-47, 129
De Veritate (Herbert), 17
Diderot, Denis, 46
Double Dealer, The (Congreve), 147
Drake, Sir Francis, 16
Dryden, John, 30, 146, 154-55

Earle, John, 21
Elements (Euclid), 19, 36, 38, 45
Elenchus Geometriae Hobbiana (Wallis), 25
Empedocles, 134
Epicurus, 110
Essay Concerning Human Understanding, An (Locke), 144
Etherege, Sir George, 150-51
ethics, 41-42, 53, 60-61
Evelyn, John, 30

fall of man, the, 93
Fell, Dr. John, 29
Filmer, Sir Robert, 69
French Academy, The (la Primaudaye), 55
Fuller, Thomas, 17

Galilei, Galileo, 18-20, 22, 39, 46, 129
Gassendi, Pierre, 20
Gay, John, 135
Godolphin, Francis, 98
Godolphin, Sidney, 23
Goldsmith, Oliver, 135
Great Tew, 20-21
Grote, George, 156
Grumbling Hive, or Knaves Turn'd Honest, The (Mandeville), 152-53

Halicarnassus, Dionysius, 35
Hault Hucknall, 31
Hardwick Hall, 31
Harrington, James, 46
Harth, Phillip, 148
Harvey, William, 18, 39
Herbert, Edward, Baron of Cherbury, 17
History and Antiquities (Wood), 29
Hobbes, Edmund (brother), 15
Hobbes, Francis (uncle), 15

Hobbes, Thomas, The Elder (father), 14
Hobbes, Thomas: birthdate, 14; attendance at Magdalen College, Oxford, 15; entrance into the service of the Cavendish family, 16; first trip to Europe, 16; second and third trips to Europe, 18; discovery of Euclid's Elements, 19; flight to France, 22; return to England, 23-24; grant of protection by the King, 27-28; refusal of admission to the Royal Society, 29-30; death, 31

WORKS:
Answer of Mr. Hobbes to Sir William Davenant's Preface before Gondibert, The, 24, 132-39, 140, 142
Autobiography (verse), 13, 16, 19-21
Behemoth, 28
De Cive, 21-24, 35-38, 44, 67, 73, 75-95, 97-100, 115-16, 120, 122, 125-26, 132
De Corpore, 22, 137-38, 150
De Homine, 27, 46
"Dialogue between a Philosopher and a Student of the Common Laws of England," 29
Elements of Law, The, 21-22, 24, 27, 35-36, 44-73, 74-76, 79, 84-89, 97, 100-101, 105, 107-13, 115, 120, 125, 132, 140-42
"Historia Ecclesiastica," 29
"Historical Narration concerning Heresy and the Punishment thereof, An," 28
History of the Peloponnesian Wars (translation of Thucydides), 17, 21-22, 32-38, 54, 59
Iliad and Odyssey (translation of Homer), 30, 132
Leviathan, 13, 21, 23-24, 27, 29, 35-37, 44, 46, 73, 79, 96-131, 132, 154
Of Liberty and Necessity, 23, 26
"Praefatio" (Mersenne's Ballistica), 22
"Questions concerning Liberty, Necessity and Chance," 26
Short Tract on First Principles, A, 20, 38-43

"Six Lessons to the Savilian Professor in Mathematics," 25

"To the Reader, Concerning the Virtues of the Heroic Poem" (preface to the *Iliad* and *Odyssey*), 132, *142-45*

"To the Honourable Edward Howard, Esq. on his intended impression of his poem of the 'British Princess,'" 132, 142

Hobbism, 146-49
Holland, Philemon, 17
Homer, 17, 34, 143
honour, 54, 111-13
Horace, 133
Hume, David, 155
Hussee, Sir James, 16
Hyde, Edward, Earl of Clarendon, 21

Jonson, Ben, 18

Kpeler, Johannes, 18
knowledge, 51-53

Lamb, Charles, 152
Latimer, Robert, 15
laws of nature, 60-64, 80-84, 89-91, 116-18
Leibniz, Gottfried Wilhelm von, 19, 146
*Le Monde* (Descartes), 22
Livy, 17
Locke, John, 106, 146, 155
"Love and Life, A Song" (Rochester), 150
Lucan, 134, 143
Lucretius, 134

Machiavelli, Nicollò, 110
Macpherson, C.B., 111
Malmesbury, 14
Mandeville, Bernard, 146
*Man of Mode, The* (Etherege), 151-52
man's natural state (state of nature), 58-60, 78-80, 114-15
*Medea* (Euripides), 15
*Meditations* (Descartes), 22
mental faculties, 39-40, 46-49, 110-11

*Mercurius Politicus* (Marchamont Needham), 24
Mersenne, Marin, 20, 22-23
Mill, James, 156
Milton, John, 26
Mintz, Samuel I., 146
*Mister Hobb's State of Nature Considered* (Eachard), 147
Molesworth, Sir William, 156
Montaigne, Michel Eyquem de, 133
Morley, George, 21
motion, 39-40

Newton, Isaac, 19, 129
nominalism, 104-105, 140, 163n5
North, Sir Thomas, 17

*Objections and Replies, The* (Descartes), 22
optics, 40
origins of government, 65-67

passions, the, 54-56, 107-11
Pepys, Samuel, 30
Petty, William, 152
"Phillis, for shame let us improve" (Dorset), 150
Phocylides, 134
Pliny, 17
Plutarch, 17
*Poetics, The* (Aristotle), 140-41
power, 53-56, 111-13
*Practice of Piety, The*, 147
*Prose Characters* (Butler), 147-48
Pufendorf, Samuel von, 146
Pybrach, 134

Quintilian, 133

*Rhetoric* (Aristotle), 55
rights of nature, 59-60, 115-16
*Robinson Crusoe* (Defoe), 153-54
Robotham, Charles, 124
Rousseau, Jean Jacques, 79-80, 161n2
Royal Society, The, 29-30, 154

Sackville, Charles, sixth Earl of Dorset, 150

Saint John, Henry, Viscount Boling-
broke, 155
Sandys, George, 21
"Satyr Against Reason and Mankind"
(Rochester), 150-51
Savile, Sir George, Marquis of Halifax,
150
Scargil, Daniel, 29
Sedley, Sir Charles, 150
Selden, John, 21
Sheldon, Gilbert, 21
Sidney, Sir Philip, 133
skepticism, 47-48, 53, 126-29, 136
Skinner, Quentin, 146
Sorbière, Samuel, 23, 74
speech, 50-51, 103-105
Spingarn, J.E., 155
Stephen, Leslie, 64
Strauss, Leo, 55, 129
Suetonius, 17
Swift, Jonathan, 155

Table of Human Passions, The (Coëffe-
teau), 55
Tale of a Tub, A (Swift), 148-49
Temple, Sir William, 155
Theognis, 134

theology, 56, 125-26, 130-31
thought, 49-50, 101-103, 105
Tillotson, John, Archbishop of Canter-
bury, 147
Tönnies, Ferdinand, 38

Villiers, George, second Duke of Buck-
ingham, 150
Vindiciae Academiarium (Ward), 25
Virgil, 143

Waller, Edmund, 133
Wallis, John, 25, 30, 154
Ward, Seth, 25, 30, 154
Warrender, Howard, 67
Watkins, J.W.N., 42, 104
Westport, 14
White, Thomas, 28
Wilmot, John, second Earl of Roch-
ester, 146, 151
Will, 57-58
Wolseley, Charles, 149-50
Wood, Anthony, 20
Wycherley, William, 150-51

Xenophon, 17

192
H682

105163